# ANGLO-SAXON ENGLAND IN 100 PLACES

DAVID EDMONDSON

AMBERLEY

First published 2014

Amberley Publishing
The Hill, Stroud
Gloucestershire, GL5 4EP

www.amberley-books.com



British Library Cataloguing in Publication Data.
A catalogue record for this book is available from the British Library.

ISBN 978 1 4456 4315 1 (paperback)
ISBN 978 1 4456 4331 1 (ebook)

Typesetting and Origination by Amberley Publishing.
Printed in Great Britain.

# Contents

# Preface

There is a great depth of academic scholarship centred on the Anglo-Saxons. This book on the other hand has been written for the general reader and does not require prior knowledge of the subject. It is primarily a county-by-county guide to artefacts and buildings through which something of the Anglo-Saxon age can be seen. This covers churches, high crosses and other sites that are accessible to the public, and objects and manuscripts that can be viewed in museums and libraries. To provide context, an outline of Anglo-Saxon history, art, poetry and other topics is provided by means of a short introduction and information boxes at various points throughout the text.

Three caveats need to be made in respect of the book. First, Anglo-Saxon England was not the same as the England defined by present borders with Wales and Scotland. What later became Lothian and Borders Scotland, for example, was for centuries part of the Anglo-Saxon kingdom of Northumbria. Slices of east Wales were once part of Anglo-Saxon Mercia. Scotland and Wales cannot be excluded.

Secondly, 'Anglo-Saxon England' cannot be viewed as a homogeneous term. England existed as a single political entity for only the final quarter of the Anglo-Saxon age. Anglo-Saxon itself is a generic name covering the descendants of Angle, Jute, Saxon and other Germanic newcomers to Britain who, though belonging to the same broad culture, had different roots and customs. Moreover, the population of Anglo-Saxon England was far from exclusively Germanic in ethnic origin. Indigenous Britons remained the majority population in much, if not most, of the land – albeit their Celtic Old Welsh and Cornish largely gave way to Germanic Old English. Subsequently, another wave of newcomers swept across the North Sea to populate large parts of England, the Scandinavian invaders and settlers popularly referred to as Vikings. Ethnically close to Anglo-Saxons and speaking a Germanic language related to Old English, now called Old Danish or Old Norse, these people were distinct nonetheless. Over time, descendants of

Angles and Saxons, Jutes and Britons, Danes and Norsemen, became the English, but the disparate make-up of Anglo-Saxon England needs to be remembered.

Thirdly, the book's terminus is the fateful year of 1066, but to some degree it is an artificial end. Norman conquest was not the totally transforming event that is often portrayed, and the England that was fashioned after it owed much to the sophisticated Anglo-Saxon society and culture that preceded it. William I might have placed Normans and other Continental supporters in almost every position of political and religious power in the land, and virtually every native landholder might have been dispossessed or downgraded in favour of an alien nobility, but Anglo-Saxon and Anglo-Scandinavian laws, administrative systems, coinage and art continued. He might have recast a society that had evolved piecemeal over centuries into a French-influenced feudal state, but old English custom remained the bedrock. His French speech might have introduced numerous new words and adaptations, and become the first language of England's kings and court for nearly 300 years, but it never displaced English as the tongue of the people.

# Acknowledgements

I should like to thank a number of people and organisations for their assistance in the preparation of this book. Firstly, my beloved wife Lynne for her encouragement and proof reading, and my dear friend Steve Boxall of Pickering for his superb drawings and paintings. For their kind provision of photographs: Pat McLaughlin of Thorpe Salvin, Rotherham; The Friends of All Saints' Church, Brixworth; the Friends of All Saints, Earls Barton; Lillie Jenkins of Wing, Buckinghamshire; Bryan Harris of Bradford-upon-Avon; Bill Puttick of St Nicholas Parish, Worth, Sussex; AMR Coins Ltd of Leeds. For permission to reproduce copyrighted images: the Chapter of Durham Cathedral; the British Museum; the British Library; English Heritage. Finally, and importantly, Christian Duck of Amberley Publishing for her support and advice in my new venture.

David Edmondson, July 2014.

# About the Author

David Alan Edmondson was born in Lancashire in 1949 and spent his career as a town planner and regeneration officer in neighbouring Yorkshire. His interest in historical places dates back to boyhood outings by steam train and Ribble bus throughout his native county and beyond. Decades later, retirement has provided the opportunity to bring together in book form this interest in places and his fascination in the Anglo-Saxon era. He and his wife Lynne live in the Pennine fringe of south Yorkshire.

# Introduction

The origin of England, or *Angelcynes lond*, lies in the demise of the Roman province of Britannia in the fifth century. Part of a bigger story of Germanic diaspora and successor states throughout the disintegrating western Roman Empire, this is a tale of, on one hand, shadowy battles and 'proud war-smiths, warriors eager for fame', as a tenth-century poem proclaimed them; on the other hand, it is a tale of peaceful integration and tilling of the soil. Contemporary written accounts being sparse, knowledge of the time relies heavily upon the archaeology of burial sites and half-remembered accounts written long afterwards. Much is unknown or contradictory. Exactly how a northern Germanic social structure and language from far beyond the Roman world come about in a Latin and Celtic-speaking Britain is a highly controversial question. What *is* accepted by most modern historians and archaeologists is that this new society did not come about in an overwhelming invasion of ethnic cleansing and migration, as was once thought. A more subtle process of transformation seems to have taken place.

Although it would be many years before Anglo-Saxondom completed its main westward expansion, the framework of its kingdoms, under recognisable dynastic leaders who can be called the first English kings, was firmly in place by the close of the sixth century. In the north-east, two kingdoms were centred on York and Bamburgh, later to be united as Northumbria. Another, that of the *east Ængle*, or the East Angles, gave us the name that we still use for their part of England, East Anglia. Several more occupied the great swathe from what became Lincolnshire through to Staffordshire, Warwickshire and Oxfordshire. These included early Mercia. Further south, between the Stour and Severn estuaries and the south coast as far west as Dorset, were kingdoms represented by the modern names Sussex, Essex and Wessex, i.e. the kingdoms of the *suth Seaxe*, or the South Saxons, the *east Seaxe* and the *west Seaxe* respectively. Bordering the South and East Saxons was the kingdom of Kent.

The key point to note is just how many separate kingdoms and royal houses made up early England. A unified country would come about only after several centuries and for much of the Anglo-Saxon age, *Ængla land* existed instead under a system of overlordship called *Bretwalda*. Supplanting East Anglia, Northumbria gradually won this overlordship under its seventh-century kings. During the reign of King Aldfrith in the last decade of that century and the first decade of the eighth would flower a cultural period now known as Northumbria's Golden Age, much of which will become evident in chapters 1 and 4, but political and military pre-eminence had by then passed to Mercia.

Under the long-reigning kings Ethelbald (716–757) and Offa (757–796), eighth-century Mercia expanded its authority over all the kingdoms south of the Humber. Particularly by bringing Kent, East Anglia and London into his orbit, Offa made Mercia wealthy as well as all-powerful. Mercian dominance eventually waned following defeat in 825–828 by Egbert of Wessex, a king who founded what proved to be the most stable and long-lasting dynasty in Anglo-Saxon history. With the growing power of Wessex also came the final demise of Essex, Sussex and Kent as autonomous kingdoms. What had been ten or more loose kingdoms 200 years previously were now consolidated into four much more fully integrated kingdoms: taking in all the south apart from British Dumnonia (Cornwall), the kingdom of Wessex itself; stretching northwards from the Thames to the Humber and the Mersey, the kingdom of Mercia; northwards again as far as the Forth, the kingdom of Northumbria; and independent once more beyond un-drained Fens, the kingdom of East Anglia. All four were soon to face the *vikingr*, a word that roughly means marauder or freebooter.

866 is not a date as well known as 1066, nor Ivarr and Halfdene names as well known as William, yet the army of Viking adventurers that struck out from England's eastern coast that year – the *micel here*, or 'great host', as Anglo-Saxon chroniclers called it – was to scythe through the land every bit as keenly as the Norman one that stepped ashore on its southern coast 200 years later. After decades of hit-and-run raids, this time the Vikings came intent on full-blown conquest. To a large extent, they succeeded. Within four years, Anglo-Saxon Northumbria and East Anglia had fallen, their kings perishing in the onslaught – Osbert at the gates of York and Edmund to become the martyr-saint commemorated in the Suffolk town name Bury St Edmunds. Mercia, obliged to come to terms, would later be partitioned into a Viking east and an English west. In 871, with the great host poised on Salisbury Plain and a new king just twenty-two years old on the throne, it seemed that Wessex would suffer a similar fate. Fortunately, this king was the warrior, military organiser and scholar upon whom one day would be bestowed the appellation 'the Great': Alfred.

Alfred is famous for saving Anglo-Saxondom but the turnabout was not instant. Viking armies thrust deep into Wessex, reaching as far as Exeter and Dorset. Viking states replaced Anglo-Saxon ones in half of England, the half that came to be called the Danelaw. Alfred fought Vikings for much of his reign. His son, King Edward the Elder, his tenacious fighting daughter, Ethelflaed of Mercia, and his grandsons in turn, Athelstan, Edmund I and Eadred, continued the battle. This was an era of ebb and flow in which the swearing of homage to Wessex kings and even outright annexation by Athelstan, 'King of All Britain', were only ever interludes to Viking resurgence. Eventually though, up in the northern Pennines in 954, the last Norse king of York, the Eric 'Bloodaxe' much revered in Icelandic sagas, met his own bloody end.

Eric's death left a very different England to the England that had existed 100 years before. Although the Viking states had been absorbed, Anglo-Scandinavian law, social organisation and speech continued in the Danelaw. Indeed, 'law' is one of many English words that are Old Danish or Old Norse in origin. Crucially, whereas immediately before the Vikings there had been four separate kings, each with his *witangemot,* or council (moot) of leading men, one king counselled by one Witan now ruled. To cement this new reality, in 973 King Edgar 'the Peaceable' of Wessex was crowned Rex Anglorum, King of the English. Despite conquest, civil war and revolution, a single, united England has existed ever since.

Let us now return to the beginning of the story in the fifth and sixth centuries. What then remained of old Romano-British walled towns was of little use to early Anglo-Saxon society as major centres of population. Even so, in the course of time many were re-occupied for specific purposes. Durovernum Cantiacorum, for example, became the seat not only of the kings of Kent but also of England's first archbishopric, Canterbury – which it still is. Venta Belgarum became a see and royal centre for Wessex, Winchester. Londinium's trading role continued, with Anglo-Saxon coins bearing the name of London in existence by about 640 and its position as a major port well-established by Offa's time. Eboracum became England's second archbishopric and Northumbria's only sizeable town, York.

Likewise, many humble places whose name include Anglo-Saxon 'ham', 'worth', 'tun', 'leah', 'wic' or 'hamtun' gradually grew in importance. Hexham was the seat of a bishop as early as the 670s; Tamworth (the enclosure by the Tame) became a Mercian royal centre; Wilton (the farm by the Wylye) and Berkeley (the clearing in birch wood) grew into tenth-century boroughs that minted some of England's early pennies; Ipswich (*Gipeswic*, or Gip's trading place) and Southampton (originally *Hamwic*, subsequently *Hamtun)* were already fledgling ports in the late seventh century. A further spur to growth came with a network of fortified towns created by Alfred, Edward the Elder and Ethelflaed, firstly to defend Wessex and west Mercia against Viking attack and later as bases from which to advance against the Danelaw. Protected by ramparts or in some cases by repaired Roman walls, these planned towns had trading, market and administrative roles as well as a garrison function. Wessex places such as Cricklade, Wareham, Wallingford and Winchester itself, and Buckingham, Bridgnorth, Warwick, Towcester and other places further north, grew out of this process. In its turn, Viking settlement brought enhanced trading and commercial enterprise, creating a cosmopolitan

The church of St John the Baptist, Kirk Hammerton, North Yorkshire: tenth century.

and much-expanded York. The Danelaw confederacy known as the Five Boroughs likewise spurred the development of Lincoln, Stamford, Nottingham, Leicester and Derby.

By late Anglo-Saxon times, dozens of the present towns and cities in the southern half of England were already urban centres to some degree. However, in stark contrast to our Roman and late mediaeval towns, little remains above ground to tell of Anglo-Saxon and Viking towns, although street layouts and names often can be traced back to them. Urban populations were small, being measured in hundreds and low thousands, with only London, Norwich, Winchester and York probably in the 5,000–10,000 range. Add to this the fact that buildings were predominantly timber and it is unsurprising that redevelopment and expansion over 1,000 years has left little to see. There is, though, one group of Anglo-Saxon buildings that we can still see. These are stone churches.

The early English worshipped the northern gods, who are still with us in modern English in 'Tuesday' (i.e. Tiw's day), 'Wednesday' (Woden's day), 'Thursday' (Thunor's day), 'Friday' (Frija's day) and 'Easter' (Eostre, goddess of Spring). Conversion to Christianity came with the arrival on Thanet in 597 of a southern, Roman mission led by St Augustine and later, on Lindisfarne in 633, of a western, Gaelic one from Iona led by the monk St Aidan. By the final quarter of the seventh century, all Anglo-Saxon England had become Christian. Now universally looking to Roman practice rather than that of Iona, all the kingdoms were spiritually united under one papally appointed archbishop at Canterbury, the archbishop from 668 until his death in 690 being Theodore of Tarsus, in Asia Minor. So complete was the conversion that in the year of Theodore's death a Northumbrian evangelist, St Willibrord, set sail to preach the Gospel among his pagan brethren across the North Sea in Frisia, ultimately becoming the first archbishop of Utrecht; and a Wessex youth called Winfrith was embarking on a monastic life that would eventually see him acclaimed St Boniface, the apostle of the Germans.

By this time, England was subdivided into sixteen bishoprics, their episcopal churches often based on places that still function as such today, examples in addition to those mentioned above including Rochester, Lichfield and Worcester. The influence of mother-churches and monasteries on the early development of towns is also evidenced by the OE *mynster* in Buckminster, Kidderminster, Axminster, Beaminster, Warminster, Sturminster and Minster-in-Thanet for example. In the sense of 'holy assembly place', OE *stowe* is seen in other town names, either on its own or prefixed by the name of a particular spiritual person.

Examples are Stow in Lincolnshire, Edwinstowe in Nottinghamshire (Edwin's holy place, originally an oratory to Northumbria's first Christian king, close to where he was slain in battle) and Felixstowe in Suffolk (named for the missionary Felix, apostle of the east Angles). A spring or stream, *wella*, could have a sacred role, often becoming a monastic site at whose gates a lay settlement would then develop, as at Wells, Bywell and Southwell.

Many such names go back to the seventh and eighth centuries, reflecting Anglo-Saxon society's fervent first years of Christianity and its feverish building of monasteries and churches. It is in the Anglo-Saxon era that the origins of many of England's greatest churches lie, Westminster Abbey, Peterborough Cathedral and Sherborne Abbey among them. However, because these great churches are great, we are not necessarily aware of their early origin. Swept away or buried by subsequent, grander aspirations, often rebuilt more than once, of the original Anglo-Saxon buildings all that survives is, at best, a small crypt here or some fragmentary walling and carved stones there.

Christmas 2013 at the church of All Saints, Brixworth, Northamptonshire. Christ's Mass has been celebrated in the same building for over 1,200 years. (*Friends of All Saints, Brixworth*)

At the parish level, by contrast, much still exists. The astonishing fact is that upwards of 400 English churches contain Anglo-Saxon work. Mostly, this work has been considerably altered or enlarged, often to such an extent that the bulk of these 400 are not included in this book. Sometimes the entire body of a church has been replaced to fit changed liturgical requirements and growing congregations, but a perfectly adequate tower has been retained; there are dozens of Anglo-Saxon towers over 1,000 years old attached to younger churches. In a few cases though, the real jewels, Anglo-Saxon churches have survived virtually intact, or at least sufficiently intact for their ancient architecture to be obvious. As a result we can, in England in the 2000s, stand inside living churches dating as far back as the 600s and 700s.

Several dozen churches are described or mentioned in subsequent chapters. Many are open to visitors outside service times, and others are locked for security but often with information displayed about key-holders living nearby. As arrangements can and do change, this book does not include individual details. It is advisable to check websites for details or contact phone numbers before making a special journey.

Before leaving the subject of churches, it is worth looking at the word itself. Consider the following: Old English *cirice,* with its soft pronunciation more evident in Middle English *chirche*; Old Norse *kirkja*, with its hard pronunciation evident in place names such as Kirkham, Kirkby and Kirkdale (England), Kirkwall (Orkney) and Kirkenes (Norway); modern English *church* and, in Scotland, *kirk*; modern German *Kirche*; modern Dutch *kerk*. With them put together like this, we have a good example of the commonality and development of Germanic language.

Mirroring both pagan and Christian influences, Anglo-Saxon art is a heady mix revealed by a wealth of surviving jewellery and precious metalwork, stone carving, illuminated manuscripts and artefacts in whalebone and walrus ivory. Often of stunning craftsmanship and demonstrating Anglo-Saxon society's delight in complex symbolism, visual imagery and showy display of power and status, it is considered to be a high point in the early mediaeval art of Europe. Much is based on highly stylised and almost abstract animal and bird motifs and intricate zoomorphic interlace. Subsequent chapters provide a general pointer to the main collections in national and provincial museums; a few town museums are also included but several others also have Anglo-Saxon and Viking items that are worth searching out. Entries are not detailed listings of content, although notable items are highlighted and briefly described to give an idea of what museums hold.

The high cross at Ruthwell, Dumfriesshire, *c.* 700.

Stone carving can be seen not only in museums but also *in situ* in churches, churchyards and elsewhere. Particularly in the Northumbrian and Mercian regions, it includes monumental free-standing high crosses. In contrast to metalwork, where a more purely Anglo-Saxon and Germanic aesthetic tradition continued, stone carving reflects conversion and exposure to Mediterranean Christian sculpture, and is predominantly religious in nature. It generally displays pictorial themes from biblical narrative, combined with vine scrolls of classical origin and other decorative motifs. Occasionally, there is also sculptural iconography to remind us of the Germanic pagan past. Additionally, Viking settlement mingled different traditions to create what is now called Anglo-Scandinavian sculpture. The book includes over three dozen key examples of high crosses and other sculptured pieces. However, unless they have a particularly significant history or display especially interesting carving, numerous small or badly worn works and fragmentary remains of high crosses are omitted. It should also be borne in mind that what now is bare stone would in many cases have once been brightly painted.

Another major outcome of conversion to Christianity was writing and the art of manuscript illumination. In common with Germanic Europe, a runic alphabet had been used for writing ritual and other inscriptions on hard materials. This was of restricted practicality however and in the sense of 'civilised' writing in the Latin alphabet on parchment or vellum, early Anglo-Saxon society was illiterate. Amazingly then, by the end of the seventh century and the start of the next, that society was producing written work that counts among England's most important. Crucially, much was written in (Old) English as well as in Latin.

Anglo-Saxon writing is a mix of works arising from their new Christian faith and tales of heroes, obligation and origin. Much of it is poetry, particularly narrative poetry in alliterative and rhythmic form primarily intended for oral recitation. Inevitably, much poetry will have been lost but among several dozen known works is the earliest surviving long poem in English and any Germanic language. Possibly composed in Mercia or East Anglia some time between AD 700 and 750, *Beowulf* is the equivalent of about 3,200 lines of modern poetry. It is a work of heroic virtues versus evil, an epic based on semi-mythical stories and folk tales passed down through an oral tradition from the south Scandinavian homelands of the Angles, Jutes and Danes. We read of the Geat warrior Beowulf fighting to protect the Danish King Hrothgar and his great hall of Heorot from evil personified as monsters. Far away in location and time as such names are, in the likes of Rothbury, or 'Hrotha's fort', and in the *heorot* in place names such as Hart and Hartlebury, they continue to come faintly to our ears. Other poems taken from a strong oral tradition also reflect the origins of Anglo-Saxon culture. Met in *Widsith*, for instance, is King Offa – not King Offa of Mercia but a distant ancestor king of Angeln in Scandinavia.

The heroic spirit continued right through to late Anglo-Saxon poetry, although there are also more melancholic and elegiac poems. There is also a tradition of religious poetry starting with the earliest named English poet, Cædmon, and continuing 100 years later with Cynewulf. In the imaginative late seventh-century *Dream of the Rood* (poet unknown), the Crucifixion is related by the tree that becomes Christ's Cross. It will be encountered in stone in chapter 1.

Prose survives in works of religion, scholarship, law and administration, leaving story-telling almost exclusively to poets. Its best-known figure is the Venerable Bede (673–735), England's earliest historian, a monk learned in diverse disciplines including chronology, and the author of influential theological works and biblical commentaries. Foremost among more than three dozen surviving works, mainly written in Latin, is his *Historia Ecclesiastica Gentis Anglorum*

– the *Ecclesiastical History of the English People*. Born soon after the death of Bede, Alcuin of York is less well known now but as a teacher and Charlemagne's advisor, his influence was Europe-wide. His writings embrace philosophy, natural sciences and religious matters.

Another great work of prose is secular and, like the poetry, written in English: the *Anglo-Saxon Chronicle*. This is first-millennium Europe's longest continuous record of contemporary events, albeit with huge gaps in coverage and in its earliest parts reading more like foundation myth than accurate history. Compiled during the reign of King Alfred from earlier monastic annals, now lost, and other written sources including Bede, it was copied to leading monasteries, re-copied, and continued by generations of subsequent scribes until after the Norman Conquest. Several copies, with distinctly local flavours, survive in whole or in part. Even in this work of prose, particularly auspicious annals such as deaths of kings and great battles are sometimes written as poetry.

A final group of Anglo-Saxon books that can still be seen is illuminated Bibles, Gospels and other, mainly religious, manuscripts. The rich tradition of Anglo-Saxon manuscript art is revealed in books made at Lindisfarne, Jarrow and Canterbury during the early decades of Christianity through to examples made at Canterbury, Winchester, Glastonbury and elsewhere in the tenth and eleventh centuries. It was not art simply to illustrate or make beautiful, however. This was illumination in the true sense, 'to light up' the word of God. This guide concentrates on manuscript books (codices) that are on public display in England, in particular the treasured late seventh-century copy of the four Gospels known as the Lindisfarne Gospels. Briefer mention is made of some others that are not on display and available only to accredited researchers or are in libraries abroad, again mostly with restricted access. Those on public display are of necessity few in number. Fortunately, although nothing can compare with the thrill of viewing an original, even one limited to a single opened page behind the glass of an exhibition case, facsimile editions supplement what can be seen. Digitised versions such as those on the British Library website are also becoming increasingly available. Some even allow the user to 'turn the page'.

Although Anglo-Saxon and Viking settlers soon adopted Christianity and much of the art and writing of the age is devoted to Christianity, vestiges of Germanic mythology and its Norse successor will be encountered several times in subsequent chapters, often in a Christian context. As with other pagan religions, it included multiple deities. Tiwaz was the ancient supreme Germanic god of the sky, known to the Anglo-Saxons as Tiw and to the Vikings as Tyr. Wotan, known as Woden by

Anglo-Saxons, was the god of the underworld and magic, the leader of the spirits of the dead and an altogether darker character than Tiw. He was symbolised by the eagle, a bird that gave him the power to travel between this world and the land of the dead. His successor and equivalent in Norse mythology was Odin (ON *Othinn*), who subsumed the role of Tyr as god of battle and weapons to become the supreme deity. Odin's battle spirits were the Valkyries. Woden/Odin was kept informed by a pair of ravens that flew around the world every day in constant watch for news, which they reported by whispering into the god's ears. He was the ancestor of kings in both traditions, even the Christian *Anglo-Saxon Chronicle* tracing the genealogy of Wessex kings back to Woden.

Thunor, the Anglo-Saxons' god of storm and weather, was the Germanic Donar, giving respectively the English word thunder and the equivalent German word, *donner*. A god of the thick northern forest and the English oak forests, he was represented by the oak tree, and his thunderbolt by the axe. In the Norse world, Thunor became Thor and protected men from evil forces; he was also the god of law and community. Frigga was the earth goddess, specifically the goddess of fertility and child-bearing. Known to Anglo-Saxons as Frija, the wife of Woden, her counterpart in Norse mythology was Freyja. Freyja shared responsibility for fertility with a male deity, her twin brother Freyr.

The pantheon of Germanic gods and goddesses is present not only in the names for days of the week (*Tiwesdæg*, *Wodnesdæg*, *Thunresdæg* and *Frigedæg* in Old English) but also in place names such as Tuesley, Wednesbury (*Wodenesbeorg*, or 'Woden's barrow') and Thunderley. The associated lore includes the myth of Welund the Smith, also known as Wayland. In this tale the smith is made captive in order to exploit his ability to forge invincible swords for gods and kings. Lamed to prevent escape, he nevertheless does eventually escape, by flying away in a cloak made of goose feathers, after exacting terrible revenge on his captor's sons and daughter. In Norse mythology, Welund has become known as Volund, and the godlike mischief-maker Loki is a central player in many another saga. Here too is the story of the end of the world, the great myth of Ragnarok, in which the gods are slain but the universe and world arise anew under the sons of Odin and Thor.

In the chapters that follow, counties are grouped under the four middle-period Anglo-Saxon kingdoms, with a separate chapter on London. As the borders of kingdoms shifted or are not always precisely known, the grouping should be treated as approximate. Entries are given under counties as defined by the

1974 reorganisation. Places in the 'administrative counties' created in 1974 but subsequently abolished as county council units (Avon, Cleveland, Humberside, West Midlands, Merseyside, Greater Manchester, West Yorkshire, South Yorkshire and Tyne & Wear) are included under the counties of which historically they are a part.

# Chapter 1

# Northumbria

Northumbria, or *Nordhumbre*, was 'north of the Humber'. Far more extensive than the area covered by the modern use of the name for tourism and other purposes, its domain reached the Mersey and the Irish Sea. Substantial parts are now Scottish; Northumbrian territory between the Tweed and the Firth of Forth and north of the Solway Firth became part of the expanding and newly unified kingdom of Scotland in the tenth and early eleventh centuries.

## NORTHUMBERLAND

### 1. Lindisfarne

Various suggested derivations have been put forward for the name Lindisfarne. From Bede's writing of it, possible roots are *Lindenses*, the people of the kingdom of Lindsey in modern-day Lincolnshire, and Old English *faran*, which meant travellers and is seen in modern words such as seafarer. That 'Holy Island' became an alternative to this much older name aptly sums up Lindisfarne's role as the northern cradle of English Christianity and a major pilgrimage centre. The site of a wooden monastery founded by the Gaelic monk St Aidan in AD 635, from 664 until shortly before his death in 687 this remote island was the seat of one of the earliest English saints, Cuthbert, first as prior of the monastery and then as bishop at an adjacent episcopal church. The destinations of pilgrimage to St Cuthbert's shrine, these first churches were rebuilt in stone in the following century. The present monastic ruins are entirely of another era, however, being the remains of a priory built in the twelfth century by monks from Durham, where Cuthbert's body had finally come to rest. Abandoned and ruined during the Viking wars, like so many other monasteries, Anglo-Saxon Lindisfarne is now evident in stone only in the chancel arch wall within the church of St Mary the Virgin (also rebuilt in the twelfth century) and some carved stones and cross fragments in the informative priory museum. That is more than compensated for by evidence in vellum, the wonderful Lindisfarne Gospels made in the monastery's scriptorium at the turn of the seventh and eighth centuries. The Gospels are now in the British Library (chapter 4) but are displayed in facsimile form in St Mary's and fully explored in an exhibition in the nearby Lindisfarne Centre.

On the mainland coast opposite Lindisfarne, Bamburgh is very much tied in with the island's early history. The shoreline crag on which Bamburgh Castle now stands was said by Bede to be the fortified stronghold of Ida, the mid-sixth-century 'king' of Bernicia, one of the two proto-kingdoms that became Northumbria. The name itself is a corruption of *Bebbanburg*, or 'Bebba's fort'. In the seventh century came a wooden church built by St Aidan, plus a shrine to his slain and canonised patron, King Oswald. No traces survive above ground, but tradition has it that a wooden beam in the present church is the one that Bede records Aidan leaning against as he died in 651.

Lindisfarne is reached via a causeway that can be crossed only during six-hour periods between tides. The Priory and priory museum are English Heritage. The Lindisfarne Centre is operated by the Holy Island Development Trust.

### 2. Hexham

The origins of Hexham's Priory Church of St Andrew lie in a monastery built by St Wilfrid (Wilfrith) during an influential but turbulent career that twice included expulsion as Bishop of York. Consecrated in 678 and probably inspired by Italian basilica churches he had visited, Wilfrid's church seems to have been very special, a contemporary writer declaring, 'We have never heard of its like this side of the Alps.' Although superseded above ground by the current priory church of 1180 to 1250, part of it can still be visited nevertheless – below ground. This is the Hexham crypt. Small, windowless and once lit by lamps in niches, this remarkable ancient crypt with its barrel-vault roof was built using dressed stone salvaged from the nearby Roman garrison town of Coriosopitum, as presumably was the rest of the church. In the body of the present church above is another survival, the Frith Stool, alternatively known as St Wilfrid's Chair. This simply decorated stone seat was used for the enthronement of Hexham bishops from the seventh to the ninth centuries: the church became the seat of a Northumbrian bishopric soon after completion, Wilfrid himself finishing his career as bishop back here. In the south transept is the shaft of an early eighth-century high cross known as the Acca Cross. This displays the vine scroll motif that features widely on Northumbrian stonework and is probably derived from Mediterranean iconography as a symbol

*Above:* Hexham Priory: the crypt. (*Steve Boxall*)

*Right:* Hexham Priory: the Acca Cross.

for Christ, the true vine. Another survival on display is a small copper-gilt chalice, one of the few Anglo-Saxon chalices still in existence.

### 3. Corbridge *Corbrycg*

Corbridge grew up around a crossing of the Tyne close to Roman Coriosopitum, from which name the OE name derives its first syllable. The mainly thirteenth-century church of St Andrew retains the entrance porch of a predecessor church founded, as at Hexham a few miles away, by Wilfrid. Now the lower stage of the tower and serving as the present-day baptistry, this lofty space is connected to the nave by a substantial archway, probably brought in its entirety from the Roman town. The original west doorway is now blocked but can be clearly discerned.

**4. Bywell**

St Andrew's church has a grand tower. Massively built with thick walls of large stones and in its lowest stages possibly dating from about 850, this is one of the tallest and most unaltered of the many surviving Anglo-Saxon towers throughout Northumbria. Its upper stage has an attractive belfry opening of a type peculiar to late tenth-century Northumbria, as does a second tower in the Tyne valley, that of St Mary's at Ovingham of about 990. Another fine tower can be found further north at Bolam.

St Andrew's at Bywell is in the care of the Churches Conservation Trust. Bywell itself is a lost village.

**5. Rothbury**

About 100 years younger than the Acca Cross, the short portion of a high cross shaft inside the church here is very different in style. Now used as the pedestal of a seventeenth-century font, three of its four sides depict biblical scenes and the fourth is ornamented with knot work. Part of the cross head, plus an upper portion of the shaft with one side depicting the Raising of Lazarus, can be seen among a small collection of Northumbrian sculpted stones in the Great North Museum: Hancock, Newcastle. These parts are much better preserved.

## COUNTY DURHAM

**6. Escomb**

The stone church of St John is generally accepted to date from 670 to 690. Its original dedication is unknown and, unlike Hexham further north, nothing definite is known of its founder. It may have been an isolated cell of a larger monastery. Set in a circular site, it is a small church just 18.2 by 5.8 metres but nevertheless having a tall nave 11 metres in height, with five small, splayed windows high up. A tall archway leads to a little chancel/sanctuary. This and most of the building is thought to be constructed of reused Roman masonry brought from the nearby fort at Binchester. Contemporary with the building of the church is a weathered stone sundial, England's oldest (to the right of the porch and not to be confused with one 1,000 years younger on the porch itself). This incorporates pagan Germanic serpent and beast-head imagery and, following the Germanic

*Above:* Parts of the Rothbury Cross, Great North Museum.

*Right:* St John, Escomb: chancel, consecration cross and chancel arch. (*Steve Boxall*)

custom of dividing a day into eight rather than twenty-four, consists of a half-circle representing the daylight hours divided into four periods. Behind the altar is an incised consecration cross also contemporary with the construction. Apart from the much later porch and some inserted lancet and larger windows, this is one of the most complete Anglo-Saxon churches. There is a good interpretive display inside. Also in this part of the county, the church of St Andrew at South Church, Bishop Aukland, has a reconstruction from several portions of an eighth-century high cross with exceptional figurative carving.

**7. Monkwearmouth (Sunderland) and Jarrow (South Tyneside)**

The twin monastery of St Peter and St Paul was one of the largest and most important in seventh- and eighth-century England. Founded by Northumbrian nobleman and abbot Benedict Biscop, the foundation dates were 673 for St Peter's at Wearmouth and 681 for St Paul's at Jarrow. Suffering badly in the Viking wars and partly rebuilt as a Benedictine house in the 1070s, some of the original structure nevertheless survives at both sites. At Wearmouth, incorporated in the present parish church of St Peter, are the west wall and small, arched windows of a typically tall nave and a two-storey, vaulted entrance porch. The latter was heightened into an impressive belfry tower, probably in the late tenth century. At Jarrow, an original chapel now serves as the chancel and sanctuary to the parish church of St Paul, whose Victorian nave occupies the site of Biscop's monastic church; three original small windows survive high up in the chancel's south wall. Both churches contain displays of early carved stonework. At St Paul's, this includes fragments showing the vine scroll motif with birds pecking at grapes and the incised Jarrow Cross. Incredibly, Jarrow's consecration stone also survives, reading, in Latin, 'THE DEDICATION OF THE BASILICA OF ST PAUL ON THE NINTH OF THE KALENDS OF MAY IN THE FIFTEENTH YEAR OF KING ECGFRITH AND THE FOURTH YEAR OF ABBOT COELFRITH.'

That so much survives is particularly symbolic as the monastery was the northern cradle of English learning, just as Lindisfarne was the cradle of Christianity in the north. Here Biscop (St Benet) and Coelfrith, his successor, built up a renowned library of Italian books and painted panels and established a leading scriptorium: the immense Codex Amiatinus in the Laurentian Library, Florence, the oldest complete Bible in the world, was made here under Coelfrith's direction around 700 as a gift to the Pope. It was first at Wearmouth and then at Jarrow that the Venerable Bede spent his fifty-five years of monastic life from age seven, and where he wrote his many works. One of the earliest extant copies of his

*Ecclesiastical History of the English People* was made in the scriptorium here and demonstrates just how far distant some Anglo-Saxon manuscripts have travelled. Believed to have been sent to the Continent within a dozen years of Bede's death, it is now securely locked away in the National Library of Russia, St Petersburg. A fascinating historical detail in another of Bede's surviving works, *Lives of the Abbots of Wearmouth and Jarrow,* is his account of Biscop bringing Frankish glaziers over to teach the art of making coloured window glass. The earliest English glazing anywhere, recreated from fragments made in the monastery's workshops and excavated on site, can be seen in the central of Jarrow's three original windows, as well as in the Bede's World visitor centre. The latter, which is a short walking distance from the church, provides a comprehensive insight into Bede, his monastery and life in Anglo-Saxon Northumbria in general.

*Above left:* St Peter, Monkwearmouth: west wall and tower.

*Above right:* St Paul, Jarrow: chancel window with restored coloured glass.

St Paul's church, the medieval monastic remains and visitor centre are just off the A185, a short distance east of its junction with the A19; Metro station 'Bede'. St Peter's is on the A183 through Monkwearmouth, close to the National Glass Centre; Metro station 'St Peters'.

**8. Durham**

In a fitting completion of the Northumbrian story, the remains of two of the foremost figures of early English Church history, St Cuthbert and the Venerable Bede, came together centuries after their deaths. In Cuthbert's case, this ended an odyssey lasting 120 years after his body's evacuation from Viking-threatened Lindisfarne. His community consecrated a new episcopal church to serve as his shrine at Durham in 998, with the bones of Bede being transferred to it from Jarrow twenty-two years later. In the event, Durham's first cathedral stood for little more than 100 years, until a new one, also monastic, took its place. This is the Romanesque masterpiece still to be seen today.

A statement of Norman power in a belligerent north, Durham Cathedral remained dedicated to St Cuthbert nevertheless, and was likewise built as his pilgrimage centre; the Norman conquerors were not averse to venerating at least some English saints. Cuthbert was reburied in a shrine behind the newly completed high altar in 1104, his and Bede's being the only interments permitted within the cathedral for many years. Although his shrine was destroyed at the Reformation, Cuthbert still lies in his simple grave in the original position. Bede's tomb, rebuilt about 1350 and also plain, as befits an austere life, is in the splendidly airy Lady chapel. A new Open Treasure exhibition housed in various cloister buildings displays the cathedral's collections. These include, in the former Great Kitchen, its greatest treasure, the relics of St Cuthbert. Here can be seen Cuthbert artefacts including his portable altar of oak and silver plate and his pectoral cross, crafted in gold with inlaid garnets. The cross and altar had originally been placed with him in his simply carved wooden coffin, which is also on display. Exquisite vestments, embroidered in coloured silks and gold thread at Winchester some time between 910 and 916 and later presented by King Athelstan to the Cuthbert community, are the earliest surviving Anglo-Saxon embroidery in England. Other items from the Anglo-Saxon age include manuscripts and a collection of Northumbrian stone carving.

Open Treasure replaces earlier exhibition space. At the time of writing, it is under development and due to open in 2015.

The St Cuthbert pectoral cross, seventh century. (© *Chapter of Durham Cathedral*)

**9. Seaham**

The Church of St Mary the Virgin is an ancient foundation, its nave possibly contemporary with Escomb's and of similar dimensions with three similar original windows, although the addition of a much later tower and large chancel externally hide the true age of the building. Surviving in a church down the coast at Hart, near Hartlepool, is fabric of a considerably later Anglo-Saxon nave, together with some carved stonework reused in the west wall. Hart derives from OE *heort* or *heorot*, the same name as the royal hall in *Beowulf* and meaning what the word still does, a young stag. Bede refers to a monastery at *Heoruteu*, which he translates into Latin as 'the island of stags'. This is probably the headland upon which Old Hartlepool now stands (OE *pol* being added later).

**10. Norton (Stockton-on-Tees)**

The church of St Mary retains a crossing tower carried on four arches, the only example in the north of England of a late Anglo-Saxon cruciform plan rather than the simpler two-cell plan of nave and chancel. It has characteristic triangular-headed windows. St Cuthbert's at nearby Billingham has a tall Anglo-Saxon nave and a tower.

## LOTHIAN, BORDERS

**11. Jedburgh**

Old English place names interspersed with more obviously Scottish and Celtic British ones tell of the centuries when the Borders and the Lothians were part

Carved panel, Jedbergh Abbey.

of Anglo-Saxon England: Roxburgh, 'Hroc's fort; St Abbs, named for the sister of King Oswald, abbess at nearby Coldingham, itself an English name; and Edinburgh, the OE equivalent of *Din* (fort) *Eidyn*, the British name existing here when the Angles pushed this far north in the first half of the seventh century. Beyond such names, reminders of an Anglo-Saxon past are few, but not totally absent. At Jedburgh is a finely carved stone slab now housed in the Abbey visitor centre. Another good example of vine scroll with intertwined birds pecking at grapes, this is believed to come from a shrine in a monastic church of the 700s. Further north, Abercorn, by the Firth of Forth west of Edinburgh, is the most northerly site in this book. Bede, writing of the monastic church in 731 and describing it as close to the estuary that divides the lands of the English from those of the Picts, called the place *Æbbercurnig*. For a brief period in the late seventh century, Abercorn was the seat of a bishopric, until subsumed within the bishopric of Lindisfarne. Substantial parts of a high cross housed in a small building near the present church are a physical survival of those times.

## DUMFRIES AND GALLOWAY

### 12. Ruthwell

The heights attained by stone carvers during Northumbria's 'Golden Age' are no better evident than in the 5.5-metre-tall Ruthwell Cross. Although worn, its total of ten panels reveal figurative carving of remarkable quality rooted in the Roman Church. These depict biblical figures and narrative including Christ as Judge treading on beasts, John the Baptist, Mary Magdalene washing the feet of Christ, the Annunciation and the Crucifixion. Surrounding the panels are Latin inscriptions in the Roman alphabet. On the sides, panels of vine scroll and bird ornamentation are surrounded by excerpts from the contemporary Old English poem *The Dream of the Rood.* These extracts are not in Roman letters, however, but in Anglo-Saxon runic script, a reminder of an older culture. The cross is Scotland's foremost Anglo-Saxon survival, albeit having been smashed on the orders of the Presbyterian Kirk in 1664 and not re-erected until the 1820s. Most of the head dates from this time. Modelled on the surviving upper arm, it is of Anglian type rather than the ring-cross or wheel-head type on Celtic high crosses. The same type is well preserved at Eyam (chapter 2).

The cross is now in a specially-built apse to Ruthwell church; if the church is locked, a key is available at an adjacent house. The church is about half a mile north of Ruthwell village itself, where there is a small museum.

## CUMBRIA

Cumbria is a name recorded in the eighth century and bestowed in the twentieth century on the single county formed by the amalgamation of Cumberland, Westmorland and parts of Lancashire and Yorkshire. It derives from Celtic *Cumbri*, the unifying name used by early Welsh writers for the Britons not only of the west (Wales and Cornwall) but also of the north (Strathclyde). The equivalent in modern Welsh is Cymry. It was preserved in the Anglo-Saxon name *Cumbra lond*, the land of the Cumbri, and gave rise to the later county name Cumberland. Together with church dedications to the early British saints Ninian and Kentigern, this suggests that a native population remained distinct, perhaps continuing to speak their Celtic Cumbric for several centuries after Northumbrian takeover in the seventh century. Even so, Old English words for lake, *mere* and *wæter*, dominate in Cumbria, for example in Buttermere and Elterwater.

*Far left:* The Ruthwell Cross: south face with Mary Magdalene anointing the feet of Christ, Martha and Mary, an archer and Latin inscription.

*Left:* The Ruthwell Cross: west face with vine scroll and runic extract from *The Dream of the Rood*.

**13. Bewcastle**

On the site of a Roman fort north of Hadrian's Wall, this north Cumberland village possesses another marvellous early Northumbrian stone high cross. Although missing its head, the Bewcastle Cross retains its shaft to a height of 4.4 metres, all made from a single block and richly carved. There are fewer biblical figures than at Ruthwell, but the main scene is of Christ as Judge standing on the lion and adder; John the Baptist is also depicted, together with a falconer who possibly represents John the Evangelist but more probably was intended to be secular. This side of the shaft also has a panel of worn runic inscription in nine lines, possibly recording the dedication of the cross to Alchfrith, son of King Oswy and brother of King Egfrith. That would date it to the late seventh century, although the interpretation is not precise and most authorities place the cross, like the Ruthwell Cross, in the first half of the eighth century. The opposite, eastern face is entirely vine scroll with intertwined birds and beasts. The cross is located in the churchyard of the church of St Cuthbert, itself believed to be on the site of an early monastery.

### 14. Gosforth

This west Cumberland village possesses a most spectacular Anglo-Scandinavian high cross, the incredibly slender, 4.6-metre Gosforth Cross in the churchyard of St James. Unusually, its shaft starts square but becomes round higher up. Dating from the early tenth century, it is a product of Christianised Viking settlers coming into north-west England from Norse colonies around the Irish Sea. Reflecting these origins, its head is of the Irish ringed-cross type. Its ring-chain interlace, also found on monuments on the Isle of Man, is characteristic of Anglo-Scandinavian crosses. Even more so than early Anglian carving, it readily mixes pagan and Christian imagery, depicting the myth of Ragnarok and what may be either Christ's Crucifixion or Odin hanged and speared through on the World Tree. The warrior nature of these Norse Viking settlers can be seen in the ranks of fighting men depicted on the side of a 'hogback' tombstone inside the church. Such tombstones are common in Cumbria and Yorkshire.

### 15. Irton

The early ninth-century cross here, sculpted from a single tall sandstone block and complete with an Anglian splayed head, lacks the figurative carving of earlier Northumbrian high crosses and is instead entirely patterned ornamentation and vine-scroll. It is weathered but accompanied nearby by a nineteenth-century replica that better shows this decoration.

Irton church stands alone on a minor road running east from the A595 at Gubbergill, south of Gosforth in the western fells. The cross is in the churchyard.

### 16. Other high crosses

Among many cross fragments and partial shafts, a good example of vine scroll and pecking bird motif is in the church at Heversham. It is ninth-century and a survival from an earlier monastery on the site. In St Andrew's at Dacre is part of a thin shaft depicting, in fairly basic carving, Adam and Eve and Abraham and Isaac. This dates to the tenth century but a tiny fragment from a more accomplished sculpture is earlier. Bede refers to a monastery under construction at Dacre in the 720s, of which probable evidence has been revealed by excavation in the present churchyard.

## YORKSHIRE

Arriving in Yorkshire, we have come to the northernmost Anglo-Saxon shire, or *scir* in Old English. Westmorland, Cumberland, Northumberland and County

Durham did not come into existence as defined counties until the twelfth century. The shire as a local administrative unit seems to have originated in Wessex comparatively early and spread with that kingdom's expansion in the ninth and tenth centuries. Until 1974, the shire of York was divided into three ridings, a word derived from Old Norse for 'third part'.

### 17. York *Eoforwic* (OE), *Jorvik* (ON)

York's Old English name is recorded as late as Domesday Book, 1086, but it is the Scandinavian interpretation of the name that more directly influenced the present pronunciation. York was the 'capital' of the old kingdom of Deira and remained united Northumbria's only sizeable town throughout the Anglo-Saxon and Viking age. As its OE *wic* name suggests, a major function was as a trading centre, particularly waterside trade, taking advantage of the wide, navigable River Ouse. Despite this, its early medieval standing structure is sparse, the main one being the late period church tower of St Mary Bishopall. There are surviving carved stones and fragments in some other churches and a simple stone watch tower in the city walls.

A minster existed at York from the time of the baptism of King Edwin by Augustine's companion, Paulinus. Rebuilt in stone by King Oswald and Bishop Wilfrid, it became the seat of England's second archbishopric in 735. It also housed one of Europe's earliest monastic schools, founded by Bede's pupil, Egbert. It was from the School of York that Alcuin took the Northumbrian tradition of monastic scholarship and teaching to the palace of the emperor Charlemagne at Aachen. Sadly, nothing is to be seen of the lofty episcopal church described by Alcuin – it was destroyed by the Normans during the northern uprising of 1069 – and just two grave covers, displayed in the crypt, remain within the great Gothic cathedral of today. York is the home of the Yorkshire Museum, however, in which artefacts and stone carving from Anglo-Saxon and Viking York can be seen. Among them, and named after the Westmorland hamlet where it was found, the silver and gilt-bronze Ormside Bowl is a liturgical item of the late eighth century and possibly Mercian. It is elaborately embossed with animals and plants. A perfectly preserved warrior's helmet, also of the eighth century, has the Germanic animal interlace and beast-head ornamentation of earlier, pagan centuries, but a prayer inscribed across the crown shows its owner, Oshere, to have been thoroughly Christian. Also of note is a small silver boar. The personal badge of the Yorkist king, Richard III, and likely to be a visual representation of the city's name, this is hundreds of years younger than the bowl and helmet, but nevertheless takes us back to *Eoforwic*. Old English *eofor* means boar, a wild animal important in Germanic mythology and often used as a protective amulet, appearing for instance with ruby eyes on a helmet in Sheffield Museum and on the helmets of Beowulf and his companions in the eponymous poem. In all probability, the word replaced the similarly sounding but, to Anglo-Saxons, meaningless Ebor in the city's former Roman name, Eboracum – which, contrary to what might be deduced, does not mean boar.

South of York, the church at Skipwith has Anglo-Saxon structure, including an impressive tower arch, plus a simple stone carving believed, as on the Gosforth Cross, to be a representation from the Norse myth of Ragnarok, the end of the world.

**18. Ripon**

The Collegiate Church of St Peter and St Wilfrid, which became a cathedral in 1836, dates above ground from 1175 but retains a crypt beneath that is 500 years older. As at Hexham, this survives from a monastic church built by Wilfrid, abbot here prior to his consecration as Bishop of York in 678. Again as at Hexham, a description in the contemporary *Life of Wilfrid* reveals a substantial church inspired by those he had seen on travels to Rome. The crypt on the other hand is small, simple and lit from round-headed lamp niches, this evoking Christ's rock-hewn tomb, whereas more splendid late medieval crypts do not. It is still entered via narrow passageways: St Willibrord, who began his training under Wilfred at Ripon, probably walked these very passageways. Wilfrid himself was finally laid to rest in his church above in 709. The *Anglo-Saxon Chronicle* records the church being destroyed during Eadred's campaign against Eric Bloodaxe in 948.

**19. Kirk Hammerton**

St John the Baptist's is Yorkshire's most complete Anglo-Saxon church, though not its oldest. It is dated by some authorities to about 950, though by others to dates well on either side of that. The church comprises a belfry tower, nave and chancel, all built in large sandstone blocks, and retains a tall but narrow west doorway, originally the only entrance. Its windows are later, larger insertions to lighten what would have been a dark, lamp-lit interior; no original windows survive. The old church now forms the south aisle to a nineteenth-century nave and chancel, but remains the dominant view on approach and clearly of great age.

Kirk Hammerton is reached via a minor road from the A59 midway between York and Harrogate.

*Above left:* Ripon Cathedral: the crypt. (*Pat McLaughlin*)

*Above right:* St John the Baptist, Kirk Hammerton. (*Steve Boxall*)

**20. Ledsham**

Ledsham and nearby Ledston are small places in the area known to Bede as *Loidis* and nowadays have a much bigger neighbour, the city of Leeds – its name the modern form of the old name and where, inside the Anglican parish church, is a tenth-century high cross. *Loidis* was part of Elmet, a British kingdom annexed by Northumbria in about 616 whose name survives not far from Ledsham in the place names Sherburn-in-Elmet and Barwick-in-Elmet. A church mentioned by Bede in his *History* as the minster in Elmete Wood may well have been Ledsham's. Certainly, the present church of All Saints there dates back to that time, if not earlier, and has been likened to St Peter's at Wearmouth. Much of the original structure can be seen, including the narrow, tall nave with high-level windows (now blocked but clearly evident), chancel arch, a two-storey west porch that now forms the lower stages of a slender tower, and a round-headed porch doorway. Stretching over the twelfth to fifteenth centuries, a belfry and spire, a replacement chancel, a north aisle and much larger windows were added, considerably altering the appearance of the old church. Elsewhere around Leeds, the church at Bardsey also has a tower that at first was a two-storey entrance porch, but in its case the added belfry stage is also Anglo-Saxon. It is a very attractive example.

**21. Hovingham**

All Saints' church was rebuilt in the nineteenth century but retains the robust, three-stage tower of an early eleventh-century predecessor, itself a rebuild of an even earlier church. Surviving from that original church is a worn but masterful ninth-century stone panel depicting, in high relief, eight arcaded figures from biblical events including the Annunciation and possibly the Resurrection. This now serves as a reredos in the Lady chapel but its original function is uncertain. The tower has a well-preserved west doorway. Set into the stonework above is a reused cross head of eighth-century date; this has the four equal arms and flared ends typical of Anglian cross heads. Back inside the church and now acting as the altar cross is the head and upper shaft of a tenth-century Anglo-Scandinavian cross displaying knotwork and intertwined serpents. Nearby Stonegrave possesses another good tower, as well as a carved figure believed to be Thor and his hammer. A church has existed at Stonegrave since at least 757, when a monastery here was mentioned in correspondence between the Pope and King Eadbert of Northumbria that still exists.

**22. Kirkdale**

Dating England's old churches is rarely a straightforward business. In the case of the little minster of St Gregory in Kirkdale, however, provenance is particularly clear. A dedication on a well-preserved sundial set above the south door reads, in Old English, 'ORM GAMAL SVNA BOHTE SCS GREGORIVS MINSTER THONNE HIT WES ÆL TO BROCAN ¬ TO FALAN ¬ HE HIT LET MA(CA)N NEWAN FROM GRUNDE XPE ¬ SCS GREGORIVS IN EADWARD DAGUM C(YNI)NG IN TOSTI DAGUM EORL + THIS IS DÆGES SOLMERCA.' That is: 'Orm, Gamel's son, bought Sanctus Gregorius' Minster. Then it was all broken & fallen & he it let be made new from the ground for Christ & St Gregory in Edward's days, king, (and) in Tosti's days, earl + This is the day's sun marker.' When reading the dedication on site, note the use of the OE character Đ and runic p (see box). Reference to King Edward and to Tostig, Earl of Northumbria, puts Orm's purchase and rebuilding of the minster in the period 1055 to 1065. Important thanes (OE *thegen*, or thegn), Orm and his father are documented historical figures, but a further inscription records two lesser men who otherwise would be long forgotten, Hawarth, who made the sundial, and Brand, who was

St Gregory, Kirkdale: the sundial and inscription. (*Steve Boxall*)

the priest. As on the much older one at Escomb, the sundial is a half-circle divided into four main time segments, albeit now lacking its gnomon. It is worth noting that although Hawarth carved the dedication in English, all four personal names are Scandinavian in origin. Only parts of Ormr Gamelson's church remain in the present structure, most of the rest being thirteenth and nineteenth century. These include nave walling, a narrow west doorway (now forming a tall archway into a later small tower) and reused elements of a chancel arch. Decoration and an incised cross on two stone tomb slabs inside date the ruined minster that Orm rebuilt as far back as 750 and perhaps even earlier. Other Yorkshire Anglo-Saxon sundials include a slightly earlier one dedicated to Ulf and the soul of Gunwaru in the parish church of St Bartholomew at Aldbrough in Holderness. It is in the south aisle wall, originally the south wall of an aisle-less nave.

St Gregory's is in a beautiful wooded spot reached via a minor road off the A170, about 1 mile west of Kirkbymoorside.

## THE ANGLO-SAXON ALPHABET

The Old English Latin alphabet was not identical to our modern one. It included a diphthong *æ* and the characters Đ (lower case ð) and þ, these representing variant pronunciation of *th*, as in then and thin. þ, together with a character similar to *p* but representing *uu*, i.e. *w*, derived from the earlier Anglo-Saxon runic alphabet. Old English also employed somewhat difficult letter groupings such as *ecg*. This book mainly uses accepted simpler forms of Anglo-Saxon personal names, e.g. Edwin rather than Eadwine, Egbert rather than Ecgbeorht and Alfred rather than Ælfred.

**23. Appleton-le-Street, Wharram-le-Street**

The churches here have late Anglo-Saxon towers with particularly good examples of distinctive belfry openings. There are two levels of them at Appleton-le-Street, which is very similar to the tower five miles away at Hovingham. The two place names indicate locations on an old paved Roman road, or *stræt*, in their case roads out of the former Roman fort at Malton. Another Old English place name of this type is Chester-le-Street in County Durham, literally 'Roman camp on the Roman road'. They don't come much more straightforward than that!

**24. Whitby**

As in hundreds of other northern and east Midland place names, the *by* in Whitby reveals it to be an Old Norse name. Here it is *Hvitaby*, or Hviti's village, but it was not always so. Bede writes at length about a great synod in 664 that finally decided that the English Church would follow Roman rather than Ionan practices, including the doctrinally important issue of how to fix the date of Easter. He reports it as taking place in a monastery founded seven years previously by Abbess Hild at *Strenaeshalh*. On that cliff-top site now stands the majestic ruins of a successor from the thirteenth century, Whitby Abbey, although unlike the later abbey, St Hilda's was a double house in the tradition of the early Celtic Church, i.e. for both women and men. Hild's was a rich royal monastery – she herself was of Northumbrian royal birth – and several Northumbrian kings were buried or reburied here. A considerable amount is known about it from recent archaeological investigations and is told in English Heritage's visitor centre at the abbey. In adjacent St Mary's graveyard, overlooking Whitby town 199 steps below, a high cross modelled on its ancient Northumbrian predecessors and with runic verse honours England's first historically recorded poet, Cædmon, who was a lay brother and cowman at the monastery around 680. The cross was made and placed here 1,200 years later. Twelve miles up the coast, Kirkleatham's museum includes an exhibition on the nearby 'bed burial' of a high-status Northumbrian woman who would have been a contemporary of Hild. Unknown but probably also an important figure in the transition to Christianity, she nevertheless was buried with her jewellery in pagan fashion.

### PLACE NAMES 1: *BY*

Town and village names such as Whitby and Derby contain the Old Norse *by* also seen in south Scandinavian place names. For example, compare Hornby and Horby, the former in northern England and the latter in southern Sweden; or Harby and Dalby, place names in England that are also found in Denmark and Sweden. Some 500 pre-Norman *by* names exist in England. Together with other Norse topographical and place-name elements such as tarn and thorpe, they pepper northern and east Midland counties.

### 25. Conisbrough *Cunungesburh*

This south Yorkshire town's name means 'King's stronghold', evolving from OE *Cyningesburh* and later being modified by the equivalent ON *konungr.* It is not known to which king the name alludes – this was disputed border country between eighth-century Northumbria and Mercia – although Conisbrough on its earth rampart hilltop was still a royal manor in the days of Edward the Confessor and Harold II. What is known is that the parish church of St Peter encloses a minster church dating back to around 750. Externally, the church is entirely fifteenth-century Perpendicular, but inside its great age is obvious. A good guidebook traces the development of this complex building over 700 years. The church is built of local white magnesian limestone. The soaring church at Laughton-en-le-Morthen a few miles to the south is fourteenth-century and also limestone, but retains a strange leftover from a substantial Anglo-Saxon predecessor. This, a doorway and porticus arch in red sandstone, stands out starkly against the creamy ashlared walls of the rest.

**26. High Crosses**

In the parish church at Ilkley stands to full height a cross of about AD 850. Its front depicts Christ enthroned and three beasts, its reverse having the signs of the four Evangelists. Intricate beast carving occupies the lower portion of a shaft. Otley has two important partial survivals of earlier Northumbrian crosses depicting not only biblical figures but also, on one, a mythical griffin. Another partial cross can be seen at Hackness, and the lower part of an eighth-century round cross shaft with figurative carving at Masham. The Norman crypt dedicated to St Cedd beneath St Mary's church at Lastingham in the North Yorkshire Moors, which was originally founded as a monastery by the Lindisfarne monk Cedd in 654, contains the massive head of an earlier cross that is estimated to have been over 7 metres tall. Of Yorkshire's other Anglo-Saxon stone crosses, the Easby Cross is now in the Victoria and Albert Museum (chapter 4) but a cast replica stands in the small church of St Agatha adjacent to the ruins of Easby Abbey, outside Richmond. Part of another, from Sheffield, is now in the British Museum, this depicting an archer crouched among vine scroll. As might be expected, a number of Yorkshire churches have Anglo-Scandinavian crosses or cross fragments. For the finest, the church of St Andrew at Middleton-by-Pickering must be visited. Here are two small but complete ringhead crosses from the early tenth century, plus the upper part of a third on which there is a simple but dramatic carving of a Viking warrior complete with battleaxe, sword and shield. Inside the church of St James at Nunburnholme is an elaborate early tenth-century shaft depicting another armed warrior, this one accompanied by the Virgin and a saint. The church of St Wilfrid at Burnsall in Wharfedale has an almost complete cross with characteristic Norse-Viking ring-chain ornamentation on the shaft married to an Anglian cross head with knot work. There is also a group of cross fragments and hogback tombstones. Another particularly good set of hogbacks is at Brompton. A rare depiction of Odin with his raven informers can be seen on a partial cross shaft at Kirklevington near Middlesborough.

## LANCASHIRE

Contrary to what its *scir* name suggests, *Lancastreshire* does not date from the Anglo-Saxon age but came into existence in Plantagenet times. In Domesday Book, 1086, the area to the north of the River Ribble had been included as a supplement to the Yorkshire volume and that to the south as a supplement to the Cheshire volume. This probably reflected the tenth-century transfer of the area between Ribble and Mersey from the Northumbrian diocese of York to the Mercian diocese of Lichfield. Anglo-Saxon dioceses were often very large indeed. In 1974, Furness, Cartmel and Coniston on the other side of Morecambe Bay were incorporated in the new county of Cumbria.

**27. Heysham**

The old village core is unusual in that it has two churches of Anglo-Saxon date, albeit both small and one a ruin. The tenth- to eleventh-century church of St Peter may originally have been single cell; it now forms a nave to which a post-Conquest chancel and fifteenth- and nineteenth-century aisles have been added. A hogback tombstone inside the church testifies to the arrival hereabouts of Norse settlers in the tenth century. For a long time afterwards, this part of the future Lancashire was known by the ON name *Amounderness,* or Amund's headland. Atop the Morecambe Bay cliff above stand the mysterious remains of St Patrick's Chapel, an older single-cell church measuring just 8.2 by 2.7 metres. The origin of its name is equally mysterious and bound up with local tradition that claims this as Patrick's landing place following his escape from slavery in Ireland. The reality, though, is likely to be less auspicious. Perhaps it was the original St Peter's, before a less exposed one was built below.

**28. Liverpool**

World Museum Liverpool has a small but important collection of early Anglo-Saxon artefacts and coins. Foremost among them is the large Kingston Down Brooch from a pre-Christian grave in Kent, a prime example of seventh-century decorative cloisonné metalworking in gold with inlaid garnets and filigree.

**29. High Crosses**

Lancashire stone crosses include two shafts at Halton, a cross head in the parish church at Bolton and an example from Lancaster now on display in the British Museum. Three crosses at the church of St Mary and All Saints in Whalley are dated to the early tenth-century Anglo-Scandinavian period. Two, with fragments of their original wheel-heads, stand outside the south door. Distinctive spiral carving reminiscent of metalwork survives well on the wide shaft of one but the subjects of figurative panels on the other are too weathered to decipher. The shaft of a third cross, with a much later replacement head, stands a short distance away.

# Chapter 2

# Mercia

Originally centred on the middle Trent and just one of several proto-kingdoms in central England, Mercia gradually annexed the others. These other early groups included the Lindenses, who bequeathed the Lincolnshire name Lindsey; the Hwicce, from whom the name Wychwood Forest derives; and the middle Angles, who have not left a modern place name but dwelt in the area roughly west of the Fens. Its own name, rendered *Merciore* on some of Offa's coins, evolved from OE *mierce*, or boundary – here in the sense of boundary people and possibly distinguishing between early Angles and the Britons to the west. As in other kingdom names, the '-ia' ending is the result of subsequent Latinisation. *Mierce* is also the origin of Mersey, that river becoming the kingdom's border with Northumbria in the seventh century and its name meaning boundary river. Marches, as applied by French-speaking Normans to the border country of England and Wales and England and Scotland, has the same Germanic root, as also in the early form of Denmark, *Denemarche*.

## LINCOLNSHIRE

### 30. Stow-in-Lindsey

Although much of its glory is later, St Mary the Virgin ranks as an outstanding Anglo-Saxon church. King Egfrith of Northumbria is reputed to have founded the first church here in the seventh century, when control of Lindsey was disputed with Mercia. The present St Mary's originates from a time when Lindsey had been Mercian territory for centuries. Refounded in 975 as a collegiate church within the extensive bishopric of Dorchester-on-Thames, it largely dates from a rebuild in the middle of the next century under the benefaction of Earl Leofric of Mercia (died 1057) and his wife Godgifu (better known as Lady Godiva). Its design is much grander than other surviving Anglo-Saxon churches this far north. Built to a Greek cross plan with nave, transepts and chancel of equal-sized cubes separated by a spacious tower crossing, it is now cruciform due to extension of the nave. At 11 metres in height, the round-headed arches forming the crossing are the tallest surviving Anglo-Saxon arches in the country. Although still quite plain, the capitals and moulded orders in these arches show the influence of the Romanesque style then developing on the Continent. Covering roughly the years 900 to 1200, the Romanesque style became increasingly elaborate, as can be seen in St Mary's splendid chancel. Rebuilt in twelfth-century Norman Romanesque, this is a little over 100 years later than the Anglo-Saxon parts. Gothic arches built within the crossing and in front of the earlier ones carry a replacement fourteenth-century tower.

**31. Barton-upon-Humber**

The otherwise twelfth- and thirteenth-century church of St Peter has an Anglo-Saxon tower of particular interest, plus a small west narthex that may have served as a baptistry. These two parts date from about 970. Rather than the bare Northumbrian towers featured so far, Barton's is plaster rendered, the whole decorated with tall arcading formed from thin stone strip work called pilaster

St Peter, Barton-upon-Humber: the tower and narthex. (*Pat McLaughlin*)

strips. As with several other Mercian examples discussed later, the tower is thought to have been painted. The lower arcading has rounded heads reflecting the moulding of the south doorway, and the upper arcading has triangular heads to reflect the shape of the original belfry openings. The present belfry is later.

The church is in the care of English Heritage and contains an exhibition on extensive archaeological work in and around it.

**32. Other towers**

Lincolnshire has around fourteen Anglo-Saxon church towers, mostly dating to the century before the Norman Conquest. That at Great Hale has an external staircase and attractive belfry openings. Others include Clee, Marton and Hough-on-the-Hill. The slender tenth-century tower of St Mary-le-Wigford in Lincoln has a stone inscription that records that Ertig built it. Lincoln was not an Anglo-Saxon bishopric, the great cathedral there being a post-Conquest foundation to replace an episcopal church probably at Caistor.

## NOTTINGHAMSHIRE

**33. Southwell**

Nottinghamshire has a cross at Stapleford and an interesting tower with later belfry stage and buttressing at Carlton-in-Lindrick. However, its most interesting Anglo-Saxon survival is smaller and needs to be sought out in Southwell Minster. Southwell has its origin in a sacred well, a spring used for baptisms since the seventh century. A new minster was commenced in 956 to serve as a pro-cathedral within the large diocese of York, to which the shire had been transferred from the equally large diocese of Dorchester-on-Thames. Reused fragments from this predecessor are incorporated in the present Norman cathedral. Among these is a substantial lintel over the belfry access door in the north transept. Formerly a tympanum, this is a piece of intertwined carving depicting St Michael and the dragon and David with the lion. Do not neglect to look underneath.

## DERBYSHIRE

**34. Derby *Dyreby***

Derby is a Norse name that in its earlier form contains ON *djur*. It means 'deer village', the OE equivalent being *deor*. As with Whitby, the name replaced an earlier Old English one, in its case, *Northworthy*. The city's museum has some

Southwell Cathedral: tympanum to bell-tower doorway. (*Pat McLaughlin*)

carved stones and other artefacts from its Mercian days and its period as one of the Danish Viking Five Boroughs.

### 35. Repton

The *Anglo-Saxon Chronicle* records that the Viking army of Halfdene and Guthrum took winter quarters at Repton in 874, but the chancel of St Wystan's declares an even older history, a time when Repton was a Mercian royal centre and much more important than nearby Northworth. Beneath the chancel, and mostly dug in below ground level, is a crypt some 1,200 years old. This is the shrine of the saint to whom the church is dedicated and whom the north Mercian place name Wistanstow, 'Wystan's holy place', also commemorates. Chancel and crypt date from the first decades of the ninth century but utilise a monastic site and crypt of late seventh-century date. King Ethelbald of Mercia was probably interred here after his assassination in 757. The subsequent church and remodelled crypt are considered to be the work of King Wiglaf, who died in 839. Wystan, Wiglaf's murdered grandson, is recorded as being interred in the crypt ten years later. The crypt is divided into nine tiny vaulted spaces by banded pillars and semi-pillars, the whole being claustrophobic but atmospheric. Some evidence of the original nave survives but the main body of the church is thirteenth- to fifteenth-century, when new windows were also inserted in the chancel.

*Above left:* St Wystan, Repton: the crypt. (*Steve Boxall*)

*Above right:* The Eyam Cross. (*Pat McLaughlin*)

**36. Eyam and Bakewell**

The churchyards here, respectively those of St Lawrence's and All Saints', possess two examples of a good grouping of late eighth- to early ninth-century Peak District high crosses that also includes part of a shaft at Hope (*Hop*). That at Eyam is the most complete and ranks as one of the best Anglo-Saxon crosses in Mercia and England. St Lawrence's may not, however, be its original location as, for part of its life at least, it stood on nearby moors. It retains an intact Anglian cross head with markedly flared and square-ended arms, this atop a truncated shaft. The whole now stands to a height of 2.4 metres, but originally was taller. The head has much figurative carving depicting angels above the Virgin and Child. Vine scroll and interlace decorate the entire shaft. Inside the church is a simple stone font, possibly also ninth century. Bakewell's cross no longer has its head but about 2.4 metres of the shaft remains. It has vine scroll very similar to Eyam's, and one face entirely devoted to Biblical scenes. Somewhat surprisingly, but not for the only time in Anglo-Saxon Christian carving, Woden also makes an appearance. Although weathered, the cross is deciphered in a comprehensive interpretive display inside the church. Inside too is a display of carved stones from several centuries, including examples from a predecessor Anglo-Saxon church. Back in the churchyard, the shaft of a second, later cross is well worth studying. The *Anglo-Saxon Chronicle* records Bakewell being fortified by Edward the Elder in 924.

### 37. Wirksworth

The church of St Mary incorporates an important piece of late eighth- to early ninth-century Mercian stone carving, as well as other interesting pieces. The Wirksworth Stone is believed to have been the cover to a grave or part of a sarcophagus of considerable importance, possibly a saint's. It depicts the funeral of the Virgin Mary, the Ascension and other biblical events. For a full interpretation of the relief, the church guidebook is invaluable.

### 38. The 'lows'

Perusal of a map of the Peak District and its surroundings will reveal many place and topographical names ending in low, often in apparent contradiction of a hill-side or summit location. Low in this context derives from OE *hlaw*, or burial mound. One such place is the parish of Drakelow in the Trent Valley. Approach it with caution, for Drakelow is *dracan hlaw*, the dragon's mound. Bear in mind that even the great warrior Beowulf ultimately fell in combat with a dragon that had seized a burial mound and its treasure.

## CHESHIRE

### 39. Sandbach

Two high crosses dominate the cobbled market place, one nearly 5 metres tall and the other 3.3, raised on a later stone plinth. They are elaborately carved with decoration and religious themes, including the Adoration of the Magi, the Transfiguration, the Road to Calvary and the signs of the four Evangelists, plus human figures and real and mythical animals. Rougher in execution than the Northumbrian Bewcastle and Ruthwell crosses, they are nevertheless outstanding examples. Their heads, possibly similar to that at Eyam, are fragmentary. The crosses are generally dated to the first half of the ninth century but have also been dated further back. Whichever, their existence is especially remarkable as

The high crosses, Sandbach market square.

they, like the Ruthwell Cross, had been broken up by iconoclasts, in their case at the English Reformation. Amazingly, the fragments, scattered far and wide for building and ornamentation, were brought together and reassembled in 1816. Elsewhere, a cross head inside the church of St Oswald at Winwick near Warrington (until 1974 in Lancashire) survives only partially but is one of the largest anywhere. The depiction of the killing of Isaiah on the end of one of its arms is a most unusual subject.

### 40. Chester

The city's name is a straightforward rendition of OE *ceaster* but could have been longer. At first it was *Legaceaster*, as recorded by Bede. This means 'Legion's fort', the fortress of the Roman Twentieth Legion in fact. Had that name persisted, perhaps becoming Leachester, it would be the English equivalent of the Welsh town Caerleon, 'fort of the Legion' (the Second in its case). No doubt that would have caused much confusion as the city stands on the River Dee, not the River Lea. The *Anglo-Saxon Chronicle* records Chester being repaired and garrisoned against Viking Northumbria in 907. Reflecting the borough's subsequent role as a major mint, the collection of Anglo-Saxon and Norman silver pennies in the Grosvenor Museum is of national importance. Chester Cathedral was formerly the eleventh-century Abbey of St Werburgh, itself a replacement of an earlier monastery dedicated to this little-known Mercian saint.

### PLACE NAMES 2: *CHESTER*

Anglo-Saxons often used the word *ceaster* or *cæster* when naming former Roman towns and forts. From this are derived over seventy 'caster', 'chester', 'cester', 'caister' and 'xeter' place names and name components (usually endings) in England. As an example, Roman Noviomagus, or 'Newmarket', became South Saxon *Cissaesceastre*, or 'Cissa's Roman camp', and ultimately Chichester. It became one of Alfred's fortified boroughs. Aquae Sulis was also given a *ceaster* name, but an Old English word that has remained unaltered into modern English soon took over as an appropriately descriptive name for the place – Bath. Several other places, including both London and York, have lost their *ceaster* suffix, while in other cases the word has mutated into 'castle', e.g. in Horncastle, Bewcastle and Castleford. (Not all castle town names are so derived, the several Newcastles, for example, being younger names that mean what they say.) The Welsh equivalent of *ceaster*, from the same Latin root, is *caer* and its Anglicised derivative *car*, although the different structure of Celtic languages makes it the initial component in a compound name. In England, Carlisle (*Caerluel*) has this Welsh name form.

## STAFFORDSHIRE

### 41. Lichfield *Lyccidfeld*

Construction of the present Cathedral of St Mary and St Chad began in 1195, but Lichfield's role as the seat of a bishop stretches back at least another 528 years. Chad, Mercia's third bishop, is recorded as establishing his see here in 667, although the Mercian bishopric – the kingdom's first – was probably located at Lichfield from the outset. Along with Cuthbert, Wilfrid and his brother Cedd, Chad began his career as a Lindisfarne monk. Of Chad's church and the subsequent cathedral that stood here from 700, all that survives other than buried foundations is a small but beautiful sculpted relief of the archangel Gabriel. Dated to around 800 and discovered buried beneath the nave floor in 2003, the carving is in exceptional condition due to having lain buried for over 1,000 years. It may have been part of a painted stone shrine that replaced an earlier wooden one, St Chad's shrine having become a major pilgrimage destination by the eighth century. The cathedral contains another special treasure from these years, an illuminated manuscript known as the St Chad Gospels. This early codex contains the Gospels of Matthew and Mark and part of Luke's; a second one with the rest of the Gospel of Luke and that of John, now lost, was listed among the treasures of the cathedral in 1345. The book has been dated to about 730. It has over 200 vellum pages, with delicate coloured illumination. They are smaller than those of the Lindisfarne Gospels, while the interlace of the carpet pages are an even more vivid display of writhing beasts and long-necked birds than in its northern counterpart and the two surviving depictions of Apostles, St Luke and St Mark, are much more stylised. Nonetheless, in view of Chad's links to Lindisfarne and other clues, it is thought possible that the book was a product of the Lindisfarne scriptorium and made specifically for service at his Lichfield shrine. That said, the book's origin and purpose are by no means definite; production at a scriptorium in Mercia itself, possibly the monastery at Peterborough, is another favoured suggestion. Further mystery is added by the fact that for a time in the ninth and early tenth centuries, the book was in use in a church at Llandeilo, Carmarthenshire, as an inserted inscription in Old Welsh records.

The Gospels and the Angel are displayed in exhibition cases in the Chapter House.

### 42. Stoke-on-Trent

In 2010, the Potteries Museum at Stoke and the City Museum and Art Gallery, Birmingham, became the joint permanent home for the hugely important Staffordshire Hoard discovered near Lichfield the year before. A subsidiary find was made in 2012. The hoard comprises nearly 1,600 main items, over 1,400 made of gold and silver, plus numerous tiny pieces. It is thought to have been buried in the second half of the seventh century. Some items are damaged and crushed, and many are fragmentary, but the find revealed one of the most significant assemblages of early Anglo-Saxon precious metalwork so far known. Much is cloisonné work in gold and finely cut inlaid garnets, a form of craft that has its origins in fifth-century Hunnic and Germanic Europe and also includes the Sutton Hoo royal grave goods in the British Museum (chapter 4) and the St Cuthbert pectoral cross and the Kingston Down Brooch (chapter 1). Intricate interlaced biting animals and boar and eagle motifs decorate other pieces. In contrast to Sutton Hoo, the Staffordshire items are almost exclusively martial in nature, especially hilts, pommels and other sword adornments, helmet plates, fastenings and shield decorations. Among them, however, are Christian crosses including a folded processional cross. Why the hoard was buried is not yet understood, and may never be. Pagan Germanic societies are known to have ritually buried treasures. In *Beowulf*, 'heirlooms and plated gold, all that part of the treasure worthy of hoarding,' are returned to Earth, from whom 'strong men first quarried them'. More prosaically, it may be a form of royal wealth, perhaps war booty or tribute, and intended to reward followers but for some reason never fully recovered. The crude way in which many of the fittings were wrenched from their parent weapons and cut up perhaps adds weight to the latter hypothesis.

### 43. Other sites

There are one or more high cross shafts at Leek, Checkley and Wolverhampton. The last, in the churchyard of St Peter's, is mid-ninth-century, round rather than square and decorated with cylindrical panels of ornamentation.

## LEICESTERSHIRE

### 44. Breedon-on-the-Hill

Although worn, the collection of sculpted stones in the church of St Mary and St Hardulph is unsurpassed as proof of Mercian stone craft. As at Repton 7 miles away, the site goes back to a monastery of the last quarter of the seventh century and remained in monastic use throughout the Anglo-Saxon period. The present church is the chancel of the last rebuilding on the site, begun in the first quarter of the twelfth century as a daughter house of Nostell Priory, Yorkshire. To the Nostell canons is owed the survival of the Breedon Carvings. These stone carvings are from a frieze that originally ran in parallel bands around a much earlier church. A total surviving length of 19 metres in several separate sections was incorporated by the canons in their new church. They display figurative

Parts of carved frieze in the church of St Mary and St Hardulph, Breedon. (*Pat McLaughlin*) *Above:* Female figure holding a book and flanked by haloed figures, probably the Virgin Mary. *Right:* An archangel, full height 90 cm.

reliefs in sculpted arcades and a wide array of interlace ornamentation with vine scroll and pecking birds, cockerels, lions and mythical creatures. The series is dated around 800.

**45. Leicester *Ligeraceaster***

Leicester became the seat of a second Mercian bishopric, this time for the middle Angles, some twelve years after Lichfield. It remained so until the Viking conquest in 872, when the bishop sensibly moved as far south in his diocese as he could, to Dorchester-on-Thames. The town then had to wait 1,055 years before becoming one again. Although the church of St Nicholas retains tenth-century work in its nave and two double-splayed windows, it is by no means certain that this is the site of the original episcopal church. On the other hand, its position adjacent to still-standing Roman walls in the heart of Ratae Coritanorum is exactly where that church can be surmised to have been founded.

## RUTLAND

**46. Oakham**

The museum contains a number of Anglo-Saxon antiquities from the local area. Rutland is an Old English name but it was not an Anglo-Saxon shire, becoming a county (Old French *conte)* in its own right only in the thirteenth century. Having been demoted to a district of Leicestershire in 1974, it is now separate and proudly and properly proclaims itself a county once more.

## THE CITY OF PETERBOROUGH

An extensive slice of Mercia around the Nene remained outside the shire system, being administered instead as a soke (OE *soken*). That continued long after the Anglo-Saxons and was reaffirmed by Elizabeth I. Although politicians and civil servants of the second half of the twentieth century brushed this history aside and made it first part of Huntingdonshire, then of Cambridgeshire, Peterborough and much of its ancient hinterland constitute a separate local government area again. It will be treated so here.

**47. Peterborough**

The soke's special status went back to a royal charter jointly granted to a monastery at *Medeshamstede* by Peada, Mercia's first Christian king, and King

Oswy of Northumbria. 'Medd's homestead' did not develop into one of England's various hampstead, hamsted and hempstead place names, however. Instead, the town that developed here became known as *Petreburgh*, taking on the name of the saint to whom the monastery was dedicated. Founded in 655, referred to by Bede in 731, destroyed by a Viking army, rebuilt in the tenth-century monastic revival by Bishop Ethelwold and King Edgar, damaged in rebellion against the Conqueror, destroyed by fire, rebuilt once more, dissolved at the Reformation and finally re-established as today's great cathedral church, St Peter's chequered history has left only a few pieces of Anglo-Saxon evidence – but special evidence nonetheless. The Hedda Stone is a house-shaped monument fashioned from a single stone block. On its sides are figures of Christ, Mary and the disciples, and on the roof is animal and interlace ornament. Although battered and worn, the original quality of the carving is apparent. Another figurative carving is now inserted in the west wall of the south transept, this being the site of the original Anglo-Saxon church.

**48. Barnack**

The church of St John the Baptist has a massive retained tower of similar type and age to that at Barton-upon-Humber, with pilaster strips and south doorway and round and triangle-headed windows outlined in strip work. All between is devoid of any evidence of the plaster that in all probability covered its rough walls or was probably intended to do so. It is of three stages, topped by a thirteenth-century octagonal belfry and spire. The south side has interesting carved stonework. Internally, the tower opens to a nave of about 1200 by an impressive archway. In the north aisle of the nave itself is a particularly fine sculpture in relief of Christ in Majesty that may have been contemporary with the tower and a predecessor nave. Another soke church of note is at Castor and dedicated to Saint Kyneburgha, pagan King Penda's Christian daughter, who founded the first church here in the mid-seventh century. The present church is a wonderful and richly ornamented construction of the twelfth century and later. Some earlier work does survive however, most notably a little section of a frieze depicting St Mark; in the tympanum of the south porch there is also a reused Anglo-Saxon carving, this another Christ in Majesty. Castor's St Mark, the Hedda Stone at Peterborough Cathedral, the carvings at Breedon and a frieze behind the altar in the church at Fletton are all the product of Mercia's heyday and possibly of a single school of sculptors.

St John the Baptist, Barnack: the tower.

## NORTHAMPTONSHIRE

### 49. Brixworth

All Saints' church is the largest predominantly Anglo-Saxon space that we can experience, and one of the oldest. One of very few surviving early English churches built on a major scale, its feel is entirely different from that of other churches of the seventh and eighth centuries such as Escomb and Ledsham. It gives an idea of just what must have been lost from Anglo-Saxon times. Founded in the late 600s by monks from the new royal monastery at *Medeshamstede*, the present church was begun in the next century, possibly at the beginning of the reign of Offa, and with ambitious intent influenced by the basilica churches of Italy. The nave is two-tiered, with four large round arches in both side walls and four clerestory windows above. It is noticeably wider than the tall but narrow Northumbrian naves. The arches originally gave access to a series of side chapels or chambers called porticos; these are now gone and the arches closed by recessed infilling and windows, one with a later, Norman, south doorway inserted. The tower, originally a two-storey entrance porch that was heightened in the tenth century, has an external stair turret and, looking down into the nave, a three-light window formed by nicely shaped baluster shafts turned from single pieces of local red sandstone. It is now topped by a later belfry stage and spire. At the opposite end of the church, through an original narrow arch, the rounded apse is a nineteenth-century restoration modelled on a section of surviving wall and built on Anglo-Saxon foundations. The semi-circular apsidal sanctuary is a particular feature of the Roman basilican plan and a less common survival in England than the square or rectangular chancels at Escomb, etc. Below and around the apse survives, albeit roofless, an ambulatory passage that probably served a ring crypt displaying relics. Nave arches, windows, tower doorway and apse arch have round heads constructed from re-used Roman tile bricks, creating a very attractive effect against plain white walls. The wide chancel arch is a later replacement but parts of the tile brick heads of a predecessor triple arch remain here too. The whole composition is set off by an appropriately simple nineteenth-century timber roof. Worth seeking out is a carved relief of an eagle, a bird sometimes also seen on stone crosses but also important to pre-Christian Anglo-Saxons.

### 50. Earls Barton

Within a few miles of All Saints' at Brixworth, arguably England's most magnificent Anglo-Saxon church, Northamptonshire possesses a most remarkable Anglo-Saxon church tower, that of All Saints' at Earls Barton. It is the last of three Mercian towers with pilaster strip decoration but considerably taller than those at Barton-upon-Humber and Barnack. The pilaster work is similarly executed, with both round and triangular-headed windows, but here also emphasises the sense of height. The tower comprises four stages, all rendered. The belfry stage has five-light openings on all four sides, each formed by four baluster shafts, as at Brixworth. The corner quoins of the tower provide a prime example of the Anglo-Saxon building technique called 'long-and-short work'. Apart from fifteenth-century crenellation and a seventeenth-century clock, it is little altered from when first built in the third quarter of the tenth century, with a small west doorway also intact.

### 51. Other churches

An impressive church tower, but one more conventional in appearance than Earls Barton's, is to be seen at Brigstock. The church at Wittering is of modest size but noteworthy for a monumental late Anglo-Saxon Romanesque chancel arch, one

*Above:* Christmas 2013 at All Saints, Brixworth, looking west to the tower window. Page 14 shows the view east to the apse. (*Friends of All Saints, Brixworth*)

*Left:* All Saints, Earls Barton. The tower from the north-west. A view from the south is shown on the front cover. (*Michael Scott, Friends of All Saints, Earks Barton*)

of the best. This is plain. More elaborate Norman aisle arches inserted into the nave walls provide a good comparison.

## WARWICKSHIRE

### 52. Wooton Wawen

Consecrated in 1042 on a site already over 300 years old, the church of St Peter has been greatly enlarged but at its core retains original nave walls, to which a clerestory has been added, and four crossing arches supporting the tower, subsequently heightened. Wooton Wawen is worthy of mention as much for its name as for its church. The first part is straightforward, being *wudu tun*, 'farm by the wood'. Less easy, Wawen derives from the name of the local thegn at the time the church was rebuilt, Waghn, itself derived from *vagn*, meaning wagon or cart.

### 53. Birmingham

The City Museum and Art Gallery houses part of the Staffordshire Hoard. See entry 42, Stoke-on-Trent, above.

## WORCESTERSHIRE

### 54. Cropthorne

Well preserved inside the church of St Michael is the head of what must have been a spectacular high cross. Its curved arms in Anglian fashion have birds and beasts feeding among vines, a common theme but here in a very distinctive, specifically Mercian style dating from the early ninth century. Note in particular the animal design.

## THE MARCHER COUNTIES

### 55. Offa's Dyke

Stretching from the Dee estuary in the north to the Severn estuary in the south, and separating Anglian Mercia from the Welsh kingdoms of Gwynedd, Powys and Gwent, Offa's Dyke is the longest frontier work of any age in Britain. Both boundary demarcation and defence line, its ditch and embankment would, when new, have had a combined depth in excess of 7 metres, possibly topped in parts by a palisade. That would have presented a substantial obstacle to a large force equipped with horses and wagons, or raiders seeking to drive cattle westwards.

Although mainly an earthwork rather than a stone barrier like Hadrian's Wall, the dyke represents an impressive Mercian achievement. It may not, however, be an achievement solely of Offa. Recent radiocarbon dating suggests that this was a long-term project stretching over the reigns of several Mercian kings. It still forms a major feature in the landscape. Well-preserved sections many miles long can be accessed on foot and in some cases can be seen from adjacent roads. Suggestions are listed below.

*West of Wrexham to west of Oswestry*, Denbighshire and Shropshire.
*Llanymynech Hill*, Shropshire.
*Montgomery to south of Knighton and Clun Forest*, Powys and Shropshire.
*Rushock Hill and Kington*, Herefordshire.
*Wye Valley north of Chepstow*, along the Gloucestershire side of the Wye. A three-mile stretch of this section is in the care of English Heritage; access on foot from car park on B4228.

## GLOUCESTERSHIRE

### 56. Deerhurst

The hurst in Deerhurst, from OE *hyrst*, means 'wooded hill'. St Mary's, on its little knoll by the Severn, ranks with All Saints' at Brixworth as the most complete large church from the earlier Anglo-Saxon centuries, and like the latter was once monastic. Bede wrote of a monastery here in his *Ecclesiastical History*, perhaps the first one in the kingdom of the Hwicce, and the present church does indeed date back in its earliest masonry towards that distant time. Most of the Anglo-Saxon fabric, however, dates from additions and heightening begun in the early ninth century and continuing into the tenth and eleventh centuries. Externally, attention is immediately drawn to the tower. This is over 21 metres tall and spans all phases of the church's construction. Its original arched west doorway, now with a fourteenth-century doorway inserted within it, is still the main entrance to the church. Internally, the nave is impressively high but originally was higher still, as can be seen from the old roof line on the tower outside. Despite the insertion of later medieval aisle arches and of Gothic and Tudor windows, there are many Anglo-Saxon architectural features still to be seen, particularly in the west wall, the chancel and the eastern end of the north aisle, originally a side chapel. Among the west wall features is a ninth-century double triangular-headed window with flute decoration. Opening on to the nave from the tower, this is one of the most distinctive of Anglo-Saxon windows. There is a fine chancel arch, now blocked

St Mary, Deerhurst: the west wall of the nave with double triangular-headed window opening from the tower.

but originally opening to a ninth-century apsidal east end. A surviving portion of this polygonal apse, which must have been a striking structure, can be seen externally. It has remnants of pilaster strip arcading.

Sculpted stonework includes the Deerhurst Angel. Carved in relief high up on the outside wall of the apse, this was possibly once accompanied by guardian archangels on the other six sides. Several beast head corbels of eighth- or ninth-century date can be seen on the chancel arch and inner entrance doorway. Traces of red suggest that these were painted overall, and their eye sockets and nostrils may have contained coloured glass; if so, their appearance in flickering lamp light and their effectiveness as guardians of church and altar can be imagined. The most important piece of sculpture is set above the inner arch of the entrance. This, a carving of the Virgin in an arched slab, is likely to have been a stone substrate for what originally would have been a painted depiction of Mary. She holds an oval shield on which would have been a painted figure of Christ, a form of iconography that has its origins in the eastern Mediterranean. Standing in the north aisle is an ornate font with spiral, vine scroll and interlaced animal decoration considered to date from around 800. This is an extraordinary survival, although whether it always served as a font or was fashioned for that purpose from sections of a tapered round cross shaft at some later date is uncertain.

Completely separate from the church, but only 200 yards to the south-west, is a small stone chapel known as Odda's Chapel, once part of a complex of buildings. Its dedication stone is in the Ashmolean Museum, Oxford, but an exact replica is inside. It records that Earl Odda built it for the soul of his brother in the fourteenth year of Edward, King of the English, i.e. 1056 in the reign of Edward the Confessor. Unlike its contemporary at Kirkdale in Yorkshire, the dedication is in Latin.

### 57. Cirencester area

This town's name is virtually unchanged from the *Cirenceaster* recorded in the ninth and tenth centuries. Three churches in its vicinity similarly retain work from those times. Daglingworth (Holy Rood) has three endearingly simple reliefs from an early monastic church: a Crucifixion, a Christ in Majesty and a St Peter with the keys to Heaven; this church also has much interesting architectural fabric. Bibury (St Mary) best reveals its Anglo-Saxon work internally. Coln Rogers (St Andrew) retains much, albeit heavily restored.

## OXFORDSHIRE

### 58. Oxford

About all that can now be seen of *Oxnaforda* is the robust lower part of the tower of St Michael's, the city church, dated about AD 1000. But the city of dreaming towers and spires reveals the Anglo-Saxon age in another way, the **Ashmolean Museum** collection of Anglo-Saxon antiquities. Probably the most historically significant item from this period is the Alfred Jewel. Exquisitely worked in gold and cloisonné inlaid with an enamel portrait, it bears the inscription 'ÆLFRED MEC HEHT GEWYRCAN' – 'Alfred had me worked'. It was found at Athelney in Somerset, Alfred's place of sanctuary from the Viking army of Guthrum and later a monastic foundation. An interpretation is that it is the crown of a reading pointer, one of a number known to have been made as aids to following the text in copies of King Alfred's translation of St Gregory's *Pastoral Care*. Among other items, both rich and everyday, are the late ninth-century Minster Lovell Jewel found in the Oxfordshire village of that name, smaller than but similar to the Alfred Jewel and quite possibly made in the same workshop for the same purpose; the early seventh-century Ixworth pectoral cross of cloisonné gold inlaid with garnets; and the jewelled Holderness Cross. The Crondall Hoard, discovered at the earthwork known as Caesar's Camp in Hampshire, provided the definitive find of early Anglo-Saxon gold coins. It contains about 100 coins from the middle of the seventh century, including some imported Frankish and Byzantine specimens.

**59. Langford**

The church of St Matthew has a late tower and crossing and a stone rood on the east wall of the porch. Another impressive tower, with much later crenellation, can be seen at North Leigh.

## BUCKINGHAMSHIRE

**60. Wing**

At Wing is an Anglo-Saxon church that counts among the most important not only in Mercia but in all England. Originally serving as a minster for an extensive area, All Saints' is a rare survival combining aisled nave and, standing above an earlier crypt, a tall and rounded – or, more accurately, polygonal – apse. As few Anglo-Saxon apsidal sanctuaries and crypts survive, to be able to see one of each in a single building is extremely fortunate. In contrast to the square crypts at

All Saints, Wing: the apse, showing the arcading, original high-level windows, ground-level lights to the crypt and inserted Gothic windows. (*Lillie Jenkins*)

Hexham, Ripon and Repton, the one here is octagonal. It is the oldest part of the church, has a vaulted roof supported by masonry pillars, all roughly formed, and is 4 metres wide at the extremes. The crypt is now accessed from outside, but originally by passageways from inside. Externally, the exposed upper walls of the crypt and the walls of the apse above have narrow pilasters forming a decorative arcade with rounded heads. Inside, the chancel arch, at 6.7 metres, may be the widest Anglo-Saxon arch in existence, though it is possible that there were multiple arches that were removed at a later time to widen the opening, as at Brixworth. Above the arch is a double window with arched heads constructed of Roman bricks. Several more original small windows and doorways are now all blocked. All Saints' crypt is probably eighth-century, the chancel, apse and nave walls ninth-century and the north aisle and round-headed arches to the aisles tenth- to eleventh-century. The west tower, south aisle, Gothic windows in the apse and other remodelling are mainly fourteenth- to sixteenth-century and tend externally to mask the true age of the building, so this is another church that has to be entered in order to fully appreciate its Anglo-Saxon core.

## HERTFORDSHIRE

### 61. St Albans

Originally named *Waclingceaster* after the folk grouping that settled around it, the old Roman town of Verulanium was never much built over by Anglo-Saxons, or indeed by anyone since. They did dedicate a church to St Michael among the ruins of the basilica and forum, the tenth-century nave and chancel walls of which form the core of the church seen today. More significantly, during the eighth century they built a monastery outside the old city walls. This was the reputed site of the killing of third-century Christian martyr Alban, and in all probability the site of an earlier Romano-British church. The grand abbey church and cathedral now on the site has a few baluster shafts from that Anglo-Saxon monastery, reused in the arcade of its south transept, but it was the monastery's dedication to Alban that had the more far-reaching effect. By also taking on the saint's name, the town that developed around the monastery in the tenth and eleventh centuries became, like Bath, a place that otherwise would have a *ceaster* name today. As with the former Roman road Watling Street, which name is derived from the same Old English root, that might have been something like Watlinchester or Watlingster. It is a name of a totally different type to that of the county town, Hertford. That name, deriving from OE *heort*, records that deer used to ford the River Lea at this point.

## BEDFORDSHIRE

### 62. Clapham

Although now dedicated to a later saint, the church of St Thomas of Canterbury is an old foundation and retains a particularly tall and massive Anglo-Saxon tower. This may have served a defensive or watchtower role. There was also an Anglo-Saxon church at adjacent Bedford, the nave of which now serves as chancel and choir to St Merton's. Bedford is 'Beda's ford', i.e. a river ford named for a person as distinct from the animal crossings at Oxford and Hertford.

## CAMBRIDGESHIRE

### 63. Great Paxton

Huntingdonshire, or *Huntanduscir*, existed for over 1,000 years, until the stroke of a pen consigned it to history and in 1974 an enlarged Cambridgeshire took over. As a consequence, Holy Trinity at Great Paxton is now a Cambridgeshire church. It is a large and important late Anglo-Saxon church. A cruciform building, it is complete with arcaded nave, sizeable crossing arches, transepts and chancel. Although considerably altered by Gothic features, as at Stow in Lincolnshire it shows the influence of the Romanesque style developing on the Continent during the tenth and eleventh centuries. This is especially apparent in the pillars and capitals of the arcade and crossing arches and in the simplicity of treatment in comparison to the later Norman Romanesque style. The original crossing tower was replaced by a steeple at the west end in the fourteenth century. Internally, all is rendered and white.

### 64. Cambridge *Grantabrycg*

Cambridge has the oldest surviving Anglo-Saxon structure in the original shire, this the tower and tower arch of St Benet's. Here is a good example of the strength and solidity that warranted so many Anglo-Saxon church towers being kept throughout England. It is late tenth-century. The Fitzwilliam Museum possesses an important collection of Anglo-Saxon pennies, displayed in Gallery 32 and also on-line. Anglo-Saxon manuscripts in the keeping of Cambridge University and Corpus Christi libraries include the earliest surviving copy of Bede's *Ecclesiastical History of the English People*, probably made within two years of his death in 735, and the earliest complete version of the *Anglo-Saxon Chronicle*, which was started at Winchester in 891. They are not on general public display but may be added to the growing digital library in due course.

## COINS IN THE ANGLO-SAXON AGE

Native Anglo-Saxon coins began to appear around 620 to 630. They were tiny and mysterious, minted first in gold and later in silver. The silver ones are now sometimes referred to by a name we still know and use – pennies. However, the penny is better dated to around 760–780, when a major re-coinage introduced a larger coin on which a monarch's name and title (or sometimes an archbishop's) would henceforth always appear. The name itself, *penig*, also first appears in eighth-century documents. The new coin's introduction is down to King Offa, for he wielded the power to make it almost universal. With few exceptions, every subsequent king of Mercia, Kent, East Anglia and Wessex issued pennies in their name. Danish East Anglia and Danish and Norse York also took to issuing silver pennies, the last often with Thor's symbol, a hammer, on them. In effect, the penny was a successor to the similarly sized Roman silver denarius – hence 'd' as an abbreviation for penny. Alfred standardised its weight at 24 grains of silver, equating to 1/240 part of a troy pound of silver. Hence prior to decimalisation in 1971, there were 240 pennies to the pound. (A single coin of pound value did not exist until 1489.) Gradually diminishing in size and weight over the centuries, the silver penny survived until 1800, the penny thereafter becoming a base metal coin. Although for general circulation the penny was revalued upwards in 1971, to 100 to £1, non-circulating pennies of the old nominal face value and made of sterling silver continue to be minted for the annual Maundy Money distribution. That makes the penny one of the world's oldest continuous denominations.

Silver penny of King Edmund of Wessex, 939–946. (*AMR Coins*)

# Chapter 3

# East Anglia

The kingdom of the *East Ængle* gave us not only the regional name East Anglia but also the county names Norfolk and Suffolk (*Nordfolc* and *Suthfolc*, i.e. the north folk and the south folk). Beyond its southern border lay the kingdom of the *East Seaxe*, the East Saxons, from whom is derived the county name Essex. In late Anglo-Saxon times, Norfolk, Suffolk and Essex comprised the Earldom of East Anglia, one of five earldoms into which newly-unified England was subdivided. This was the most densely populated part of Anglo-Saxon England, and of England well into the later medieval period.

## NORFOLK

### 65. Round towers

Norfolk has 118 round church towers, plus ten in ruins, Suffolk another thirty-eight and Essex seven (*Harris's Guide to Churches and Cathedrals*, 2006). Built of flint and small stones, round towers were a response to a local lack of larger stone suitable for the quoin stones needed to give strength to square corners. They belong to a tradition also seen in geologically similar Schleswig-Holstein. Built over several centuries, from as early as AD 900, they span pre- and post-Conquest years. It is not always possible to divide them, and in any event 1066 is not particularly relevant in this context as established practice continued virtually unaltered. In addition, many appear to be a mix of Anglo-Saxon lower stages and later upper stages, with subsequent insertion of windows also taking place. Among a sizeable number of Norfolk examples that are considered to be wholly or largely pre-Conquest are the towers at Bessingham, Beachamwell, Gissing, Hadiscoe, Howe and Colney. Foncett St Peter is a particularly good example, with belfry opening and circular window openings of typical Anglo-Saxon style. That at delightfully named Little Snoring retains evidence of its original parent church but now stands detached from the present post-Conquest one. The little-altered tower at East Lexham may be the oldest of all. Great Dunham has a rare (for East Anglia) square Anglo-Saxon tower. The west door is triangular-headed.

### 66. Norwich *Nordwic*

The county town has three round towers, including that of the church of St Etheldreda. The Castle Museum contains a good selection of East Anglian coins and other artefacts. The Larling Plaque, a fragment of a carved whalebone box from before AD 800, depicts the wolf suckling Romulus and Remus. Inclusion of this foundation myth from ancient Rome, which also appears on coins and pendants, suggests that East Anglian kings, like many Germanic kings, saw themselves as the heirs of Rome.

## SUFFOLK

### 67. Sutton Hoo

South farm (*suth tun*) on the spur of land (*hoh*) might sound an unprepossessing place but is nevertheless famous as the site of the greatest Anglo-Saxon archaeological find ever made, and one of the most important discoveries from first millennium Europe as a whole. This is the ship burial excavated here just prior to the outbreak of World War Two. As with the description of the hero's send-off to the afterlife in *Beowulf*, the burial provides a clear reminder of England's origin in a Germanic and pagan north Europe. Indeed, at Uppsala in eastern Sweden and at Sutton Hoo in eastern England are the major examples of sixth- and seventh-century ship burial. The practice may have been part of the cult of Frija and, in the subsequent Viking age in Scandinavia, of Freyja. That at Sutton Hoo is generally associated with the East Anglian royal dynasty, the Wuffingas, who are thought to have had their centre at nearby Rendlesham. Specifically, it is linked to the powerful king and *bretwalda* Redwald, who according to Bede died around 624 or 625. However, there is no totally conclusive evidence as to whose funerary monument this was and other contenders from East Anglia and Essex at roughly this period cannot be ruled out.

Whatever the uncertainties about the occupant, what is beyond doubt is the magnificence of his burial goods, now mostly housed in the British Museum (see entry in the next chapter). Although the burial ship itself had long since decayed, a perfect imprint of its riveted wooden framework and clinker construction was preserved in the compacted sandy soil of the burial mound. A further testament to the occupant's status, this is the largest known vessel from the period and, at 27 metres long, unmatched in size by any known Viking ship until the eleventh century. An exhibition centre at the site, above the River Deben, recreates the burial as it might have looked when new and presents information on the findings of the excavation and later investigations in the rest of this royal burial complex. Sutton Hoo is by no means the only excavated Anglo-Saxon burial site that has given up grave goods, but as the practice of interring grave goods with the deceased faded away later in the seventh century, it is one of the last and definitely the most spectacular.

The Sutton Hoo estate and visitor centre is a National Trust property.

**68. Bury St Edmunds**

Another place name different in nature from the more usual name types inherited from Anglo-Saxon England, this one commemorates the last king of East Anglia and England's first patron saint, Edmund. So do twenty-seven church dedications in Suffolk and Norfolk alone. Venerated as a Christian martyr and canonised, Edmund was eventually reinterred in 925 at a monastery in *Beadricesworth*. By the end of the century, however, pilgrims would consider themselves as arriving *Sancte Eadmundes Byrig*, or 'at St Edmund's Borough'. That word order reversed in later centuries, although the diocese based on the city since 1914 is St Edmundsbury and Ipswich. Nothing of the original monastery or of Edmund's tomb remains, while its Norman successor is mostly gone down to foundation level. On the other hand, the much later St Edmundsbury Cathedral, located within the great abbey precinct, does have a chapel dedicated to Edmund, so continuing 1,100 years of veneration.

## PLACE NAMES 3: *BURY*

The Germanic word *burh* or *burg* meant fortified place or stronghold, with dative *byrig* meaning 'at the fortified place'. From these are derived numerous 'brough', 'burgh', 'borough' and 'bury' place names and name components in England and southern Scotland. They are found far and wide, from Glastonbury in Somerset to Aldeburgh in Suffolk, and from Richborough in Kent to Rothbury in Northumberland and Roxburgh in the Borders. Some burgs were new foundations, such as Shaftesbury and Eddisbury, two of the fortified towns from the Viking wars. Others, such as Burgh Castle in Norfolk and Richborough and Canterbury, were former Roman towns or forts. Yet more were reoccupied Iron Age hill forts. At *Cadaesburh* –

Cada's stronghold, or as it is now known, Cadbury Castle in Somerset – an Anglo-Saxon stone rampart was added more than 1,000 years after the hill fort was first raised. Further east by then, Ægel's hill fort had already begun to develop into a town. It became Aylesbury. Not all such names date as far back as the Anglo-Saxon age and to further complicate matters, some are derived from a different OE word, *beorg*, which means barrow.

**69. Herringfleet**

Probably of early eleventh-century date and having triangular-headed belfry openings, the round tower of St Margaret's is a good example of the type. Otherwise, Suffolk does not have a great deal of surviving Anglo-Saxon structure, despite East Anglia being renowned for its medieval churches. The short nave of St Peter's, Claydon, is an exception, albeit altered and dominated by a later tower and large nineteenth-century chancel. St Peter's is a redundant church now in the care of the Churches Conservation Trust.

## ESSEX

St Botolph, Hadstock: south doorway and original oak door. (*Steve Boxall*)

**70. Hadstock**

OE *stoc* means place, the full origin of this name being Hada's place. The impressive cruciform church is dedicated to St Botolph, a seventh-century East Anglian monk. It dates at its core to the early eleventh century but incorporates walling from an older church that may have been Botolph's burial place. It is sometimes equated with the minster that the *Anglo-Saxon Chronicle* records as being consecrated in 1020 by King Canute for the souls of the men of both sides who had been slain in the battle of *Assandun* four years previously. *Assandun*, 'the hill of ash trees', was the last of four battles between Canute and King Edmund II. Here, as the *Chronicle* ruefully records, fell all the flower of the English nation.

*Assandun* has been identified as either nearby Ashdon or, further south in the county, Ashingdon. If the former interpretation is correct, that could place the battle on the high ground running between Hadstock and Ashdon village. Whether St Botolph's is Canute's minster or not, its size and architecture suggests more than a simple local church. On approaching it, the eleventh-century building becomes very obvious against the much later tower, rebuilt chancel and inserted Gothic transept window. It has a typically narrow but tall Anglo-Saxon form and retains four of its original high-level double-splayed windows. The doorway arch and the transept pillars of the crossing arches have palmette carving. The doorway contains the original wooden door, the oldest working door in the country. The partly rebuilt crossing arches carried a central tower until this collapsed and was replaced by the present west tower. Not far away in this northern tip of Essex, the church at Strethall has a small nave of the reign of Edward the Confessor and a fine chancel arch.

## THE DANISH CONQUEST

One of Anglo-Saxon England's longest-reigning kings was Ethelred II. Sadly for the country, this king was doomed to go down in history as anything but the 'noble counsel' that the name *Æthelræd* means. Instead, through a pun on his name – *Unræd*, literally un-counselled or ill-counselled – he is known to us as Ethelred the Unready. Ultimately, following twenty years of fruitless effort and a stout but unsuccessful rearguard campaign in 1016 by his short-lived successor son, Edmund II ('Ironside'), England was lost to a foreign conqueror: Cnut of Denmark. This was not a Viking conquest in the ninth-century sense of the word. Denmark by this time had become a powerful centralised and Christian state. Canute, King of England from 1017 and King of Denmark in succession to his brother from 1019, reigned until his death in 1035. His two sons ruled England in turn for a further six years. There then followed the restoration of the Wessex royal line in the person of Edward the Confessor, the last survivor of Ethelred's five adult sons. The consequences were to prove far-reaching. King Edward was a son by a second marriage, to Emma of Normandy, and he himself was childless. Therein lay the seeds of another foreign invasion of England, by his mother's great-nephew William, Duke of Normandy: the man known in history as William the Conqueror.

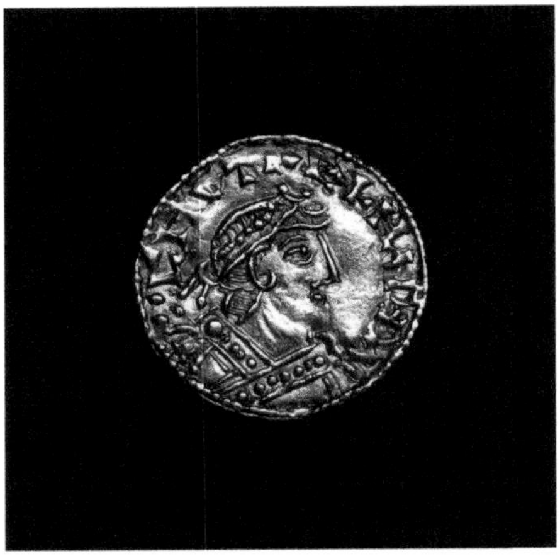

Silver penny of King Harthacnut, last of the Canute dynasty kings of England, 1040–1042. (*AMR Coins*)

**71. Greensted-juxta-Ongar**

The church of St Andrew is a mix of Anglo-Saxon nave, Tudor brick chancel and tiled roof, Jacobean clapboard tower, Victorian dormer windows and picturesque site. As if all that were not enough, the nave is wood. Constructed of oak tree trunks split so that they are still rounded outside but flat and adze-smoothed inside, the nave is the only surviving Anglo-Saxon timber structure and the oldest wooden building in Europe. Standing on a site that may go back to the seventh century, it has been dated by dendrochronology to the first decades of the eleventh. That coincides with the time when the body of St Edmund remained here awhile on its journey back to Suffolk from London, where it had been taken for safekeeping during the Danish Conquest. The nave would originally have been thatched and windowless and lit by lamps. To preserve them from further rotting, the log walls were underpinned by brick sills in the nineteenth century.

**72. Bradwell**

Unassuming, almost barn-like to the casual glance, the chapel of St Peter-on-the-Wall is nevertheless one of the oldest standing buildings in Britain. This humble, remote place is no less than the centre for a ministry established in about 640 by the Lindisfarne monk St Cedd at the invitation of the king of the East Saxons, Sigiberht. The church, which was probably started a little later, is built of bricks salvaged from the walls of the Roman Saxon Shore fort of Othona, within which it stands and to which its name refers. An apsidal sanctuary and a side porticus have gone and what remains is a nave just 15.2 metres long but 9 metres tall. A modern altar, consecrated in 1985, commemorates Cedd's mission. The bare, simple interior perfectly fits the history.

To visit is something of a pilgrimage still. To get there, take the half-mile footpath from the end of the minor road leading east out of Bradwell-juxta-Mare.

### 73. Chickney

Another Essex church with extensive Anglo-Saxon structure is St Mary's at Chickney. This isolated church has an atmospheric nave and chancel, perhaps in parts as old as AD 850 and continuing to about 1000, and an original double window. A chancel extension and most windows are thirteenth- to fourteenth-century. Holy Trinity at Colchester retains a tower whose triangular-headed west doorway is constructed of Roman brick.

Chickney is a few miles south west of Thaxted. Its church is in the care of the Churches Conservation Trust.

### 74. Maldon *Mældun*

At the head of the Blackwater is one of the earliest battlefields marked on Britain's Ordnance Survey maps. Here, in AD 991, an army raised locally in Essex stood against renewed Viking attack on England, and in doing so perished. In a rather terse annal from the *Anglo-Saxon Chronicle*, we read that Ealdorman Byrhtnoth came to meet them there with his levies and fought them, but they slew the ealdorman and had possession of the place of slaughter. In true English spirit, however, the fearsome struggle and defeat was immortalised more fittingly in verse, the contemporary long poem *The Song of Maldon*:

> Now was the riot raised, the ravens wheeled
> and the eagle circled, eager for carrion.
> There was a cry on earth.
> Then loosed they from their hands the filed lance,
> the sharp-ground spears to fly.
> Bows were busied, buckler parried point,
> bitter was the battle rush and brave warriors fell.
> On either hand young men lay.

Byrhtnoth's opponent that day was Anlaf, probably the future king of Norway, Olaf I (Olaf Tryggvason). Under King Canute and the influence of the Old Norse *jarl*, his ancient title gave way to *eorl*, or earl. It survived nonetheless until 1974 as 'alderman', the honorary title for senior county councillors. The likely battle site is at the landward end of the causeway across Southey Creek to Northey Island. It can be reached from the B1018 or by footpath from Maldon.

# Chapter 4

# London

Anglo-Saxon London comprised *Lundenceaster* and *Lundenwic*. The former, the original Roman city, is still known as the City. Lundenwic was a trading centre and market outside the Roman walls; over time, it became known as the *ald wic* – or old market – and today as Aldwych. London passed from being an East Saxon town to a Mercian one some time in the eighth century, and passed once more, this time to Wessex, in 911. Across the old Roman London Bridge and its Anglo-Saxon successor, a fortified *Suthwerca*, or 'south work', gave rise to Southwark. London became the capital of England only after the Norman Conquest. Modern London has absorbed surrounding built-up areas that were once parts of Essex, Surrey and Kent. The former shire of Middlesex was absorbed in its entirety. That county's name, *Middelseaxna,* reveals a folk grouping but not, as far as is known, a distinct kingdom.

**75. The British Museum**

The most comprehensive assembly of Anglo-Saxon artefacts on display anywhere is in Room 41, the Ruddock Gallery. Scores of other items are in the museum's back-room collections. The whole ranges from everyday objects, through stone crosses, weapons, silverware, coins, church goods, brooches and pendants and runic inscriptions, to treasures from royal burials including Sutton Hoo. Viking and Anglo-Scandinavian work is also well represented. A key feature of the gallery is its treatment of the Anglo-Saxon age not in isolation but in the wider context of first-millennium Europe.

Exhibits from Sutton Hoo include some of the most exquisite examples of the intricate and highly creative Anglian art of the sixth and seventh centuries. Superbly crafted personal adornments include shoulder clasps and a purse lid. Intense ornamentation of delicate gold and garnet cloisonné work form cellular patterns, intertwined and interlocked biting beasts, and highly stylised mythical subjects and human masks. A solid gold buckle is a mass of zoomorphic interlace created from snake and long-bodied animal forms. The eagle of Woden, widely

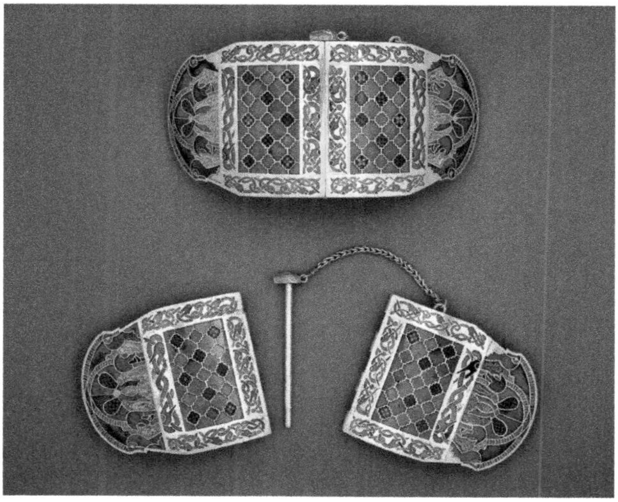

Gold and garnet shoulder clasps from the Sutton Hoo ship burial, *c.* 625. (© *The Trustees of the British Museum*)

used in the Germanic world as an amulet to ward off danger, is depicted on a great ceremonial shield, here as a stylised gilt-bronze figure. Sutton Hoo's famous helmet has a decorative and bejewelled bronze waterfowl (or winged dragon?) protecting upper lip, nose, eye brows and forehead, and another red-eyed serpent forming a crest. It probably had a ceremonial or regal purpose similar to a crown. Likewise, a carved and unusually long whetstone may be akin to a sceptre. Among many other items are a sword with gold fittings and a restored silver-mounted drinking horn. Items from the non-Germanic world, such as beautiful Byzantine silverware of about AD 500, reveal that early Anglo-Saxon England was not an isolated backwater. The whole collection reveals the exceptional status of the person it accompanied both in life and after death, be he King Redwald or someone else.

Among other precious metalwork, the East Anglian Wilton Cross is a cloisonné gold and inlaid garnet pendant enclosing a gold solidus coin of the Byzantine emperor Heraclius (615–632). Similar pendants include pectoral crosses in Durham Cathedral and the Ashmolean Museum. The Taplow buckle is a belt buckle of about 600 from a high-rank burial mound that can still be seen at Taplow, Berkshire. Together with a pair of clasps – like those from Sutton Hoo, these are shoulder fastenings for a leather tunic – it is believed to be of Kentish rather than Anglian origin. The piece is cloisonné, inlaid garnets and gold filigree borders and interlace. Taplow, or 'Tæppa's burial mound', has the same *hlaw* root as Drakelow, the dragon's mound, in Derbyshire (chapter 2). Viewed vertically, the buckle might well be a dragon's head.

Intricate zoomorphic ornamentation appears again on the Witham Pins. This silver gilt pin set from a dress is assigned to eighth-century Mercia and was found in Lincolnshire. From the ninth century comes a beautiful series of silver and niello-inlay Anglo-Saxon disc brooches. The Strickland and Pentney brooches continue the old tradition of animal ornament but here it forms cross shapes, with five silver studs representing the five wounds of Christ. Identical symbolism appears on the Fuller Cross, the ornament however being entirely figurative.

Moving away from precious metalwork, the Franks Casket is a compact but remarkable carved whalebone box made in the first half of the eighth century, probably in Northumbria. Its sides and lid are richly decorated with narrative scenes from biblical and Roman sources and Germanic mythology. These include the Adoration of the Magi, the myth of Wayland the Smith and the ascension of a warrior into the afterlife. The scenes are contained within bold runic inscriptions, one of which records how the whalebone of which the box is made came to be available: this particular whale apparently became stranded on a rocky shore. These scenes are interesting for the clues they give as to contemporary clothing. The casket is named after the nineteenth-century British Museum Keeper who discovered and acquired it. It is the most complete Anglo-Saxon casket still in England, although an exceptional eighth-century Mercian one with birds, animals and interlace is in a museum at Brunswick. This is known as the Gandersheim Casket.

Set of disc brooches found at Pentney, Norfolk, mid-ninth century. (© *The Trustees of the British Museum*)

**76. The British Library**

Anglo-Saxon manuscripts figure prominently in the library's collection. Probably made towards the end of the seventh century, the illuminated Lindisfarne Gospels is one of the earliest and the most well known. Its 258 vellum folio pages were created to honour Cuthbert and for service at his shrine at the Northumbrian monastery. It is of added interest because the names of the monks responsible for its creation are recorded in a colophon: Edfrith, Bishop of Lindisfarne from 698 until 721 and the book's scribe and illuminator; Ethelwald, who bound it in leather; and Billfrith the hermit, who ornamented it with jewels. Sadly, the work of Ethelwald and Billfrith has long since vanished, the present jewelled binding being Victorian. Fortunately, Edfrith's fine script and magnificent illumination in numerous soft colours made from natural raw materials still stun more than 1,300 years after they were executed. His work is considered the apotheosis of a manuscript style that seems to have developed in Northumbria and then spread both northwards and southwards. It fuses the swirling Germanic zoomorphic interlace and geometric cell decoration seen on Anglo-Saxon precious metalwork such as the Sutton Hoo grave goods, spiral and curvilinear decorative traditions of British Celtic metalwork, portraiture based on contemporary Christian art of Rome and Byzantium and a script style passed down from the founding Irish monks of Lindisfarne. The outcome of this cultural fusion is elaborate decorated capital letters opening each Gospel, portraits of the Evangelists as scribes and pure ornament and intricate pattern dominating whole introductory pages called carpet pages. Strangely, there is little in the way of overt Christian symbolism other than the cross of the carpet pages. Edfrith seems to have had a particular fondness for wildfowl and dogs, scores of their stylised heads terminating his interlace and decorated letters.

Another of the library's marvellous illuminated manuscripts, the Benedictional of St Æthelwold, comes from the other end of Anglo-Saxon England and the other end of the Anglo-Saxon age. Made at Winchester for Ethelwold, bishop there from 963 to 984, its illumination displays a naturalistic style rooted in contemporary Carolingian art of the Continent but still with the dense ornamentation and colour seen in earlier Anglo-Saxon art. Entwined acanthus foliage has been added to the repertoire. Together with other tenth- to eleventh-century Winchester and Canterbury codices in the British Library and libraries abroad, including Hanover, the Benedictional is the fruit of a second magnificent age of Anglo-Saxon manuscript illumination.

Psalters also span the centuries. The Vespasian Psalter is an early illuminated codex probably made at the monastery in Canterbury a few decades after the

*Above left:* The Lindisfarne Gospels: the carpet page to St John's Gospel. (© *British Library Board, Cotton Nero D. IV, f.210v*)

*Above right:* The Benedictional of St Æthelwold: miniature of St Æthelthryth. Ethelthryth, the daughter of a seventh-century East Anglian king, founded the convent that gave rise to today's Ely Cathedral. (© *British Library Board, Add. 49598 f.90v*)

Lindisfarne Gospels. The Winchester Ramsey Psalter by contrast is late tenth-century and distinctively accompanied by elegant line drawings. It and Ethelwold's Benedictional also display ornate decorated initials that are characteristic of late Anglo-Saxon illumination.

Among other British Library manuscript books are an illuminated ninth-century copy of Bede's *Ecclesiastical History of the English People* and the only extant Anglo-Saxon copy, from about AD 1000, of the Old English poem *Beowulf*. The St Cuthbert Gospel, formerly known as the Stonyhurst Gospel, is a hand-sized Gospel of St John made around 700 and placed at some later date in Cuthbert's tomb. It still has its original embossed red-leather cover.

The Lindisfarne Gospels, the Beowulf manuscript and the St Cuthbert Gospel are on permanent public display in the Sir John Ritblat Gallery. Others, such as the Benedictional, occasionally appear in temporary exhibitions. To view manuscripts not on display requires special arrangements and is normally for academic purposes.

## INSULAR ART

The Lindisfarne Gospels belongs to a type of manuscript art referred to as Insular or Hiberno-Saxon, i.e. art of the islands of Britain and Ireland in the seventh and eighth centuries. In contrast to it, the origins and subsequent histories of others of the type are less certain. The Book of Durrow in Trinity College Library, Dublin, has zoomorphic ornament very similar to that seen on metalwork from Sutton Hoo and is dated by art historians to about twenty years before the Lindisfarne Gospels. The Echternach Gospels has a known Northumbrian link, having been gifted to a monastery founded in what is now Luxembourg by the Northumbrian missionary monk Willibrord. This example is now in the Bibliothèque Nationale, Paris. The St Chad Gospels in Lichfield Cathedral (chapter 2) may be Mercian and the later Barberini Gospels in the Vatican Library is considered almost certainly Mercian, probably from Peterborough. The latter is a particularly sumptuous example from the end of the eighth century. Also a late example of the style, the famous Book of Kells in Trinity College Library, Dublin, is generally ascribed to Iona.

**77. The V&A**

The Easby Cross from Yorkshire is reconstructed from several pieces. Only the shaft, of 2.5 metres, survives. It is dated to the late eighth or early ninth centuries. One face depicts Christ in Majesty with saints Peter and Paul at his side and, grouped in round arches below, the apostles and the Evangelists holding their Gospels. The other faces have interlace and the vine scroll with birds and animals sitting in it commonly seen on Northumbrian high crosses. The V&A also has a number of small but wonderful walrus ivory carvings from about 1000 to 1050.

**78. Westminster**

When Edward the Confessor came to the throne of England in 1042, there stood in the Middlesex countryside to the west of Anglo-Saxon London a monastic church known simply as the '*west mynster*'. Originally founded by East Saxon royalty, it was already over 300 years old. Beginning a rebuild in the 1050s, Edward went on to create England's grandest abbey to date, a royal palace located at its side. Thus

The Easby Cross: part of shaft. (*Steve Boxall*)

came into being Westminster, where monarchs of England and of Great Britain have been crowned ever since, and the seat of parliamentary as well as royal government has been known as the Palace of Westminster down to this day.

The pious Edward lived just long enough to see his abbey completed; consecrated on 28 December 1065, it received his body for burial nine days later. Within the year, both of his rival successors, Harold and William, had been crowned in it as well. It was a substantial church built in the developing Romanesque style of the Continent and presumably under the direction of a Continental master mason. At some two-thirds the length of the present abbey church, it was probably the largest single building project in pre-Norman England and, as a royal foundation, much bigger than the Romanesque churches at Stow and Great Paxton. The Bayeux Tapestry shows it with a domed central tower and, like its successor, it had twin towers at the west end. Replaced by the present Gothic structure in the thirteenth century, nothing of Edward's original abbey remains visible, although the canonised monarch's body still lies in his grave and shrine behind the Coronation Chair in its successor.

# Chapter 5

# Wessex

Initially comprising the Hampshire and middle Thames region, Wessex, or *West Seaxna lond*, gradually absorbed all southern England. This chapter covers Wessex proper, plus later Wessex territories that were formerly kingdoms in their own right (Sussex, Kent and Cornwall). It also includes Surrey, originally a southern territory of the East Saxon kingdom, its name meaning 'south district'. London, a Wessex possession from the early tenth century, is covered in chapter 4.

## HAMPSHIRE

### 79. Winchester *Wintanceaster*

From a first mention by Bede as the see of the West Saxons in about 665 to its role as England's first capital, Winchester has four centuries of recorded Anglo-Saxon history and, in boxes above the chancel of the present cathedral, the bones of Anglo-Saxon kings back to the mid-ninth century. However, nothing survives of the predecessor Anglo-Saxon monastic episcopal church of St Swithun, the Old Minster, which archaeological excavation has shown to have been some 76 metres long in its final form. Nor does any standing structure survive from an adjacent and equally impressive monastery built by Alfred and Edward the Elder, the New Minster. On the other hand, the cathedral does possess the only complete Anglo-Saxon glass bowl on display in England. In its library is Bede's *Ecclesiastical History* in a translation from Latin into English undertaken either by Alfred himself or at his behest. Additionally, Anglo-Saxon Winchester is very apparent in illuminated manuscripts probably made at the New Minster, such as the lavish Benedictional of St Ethelwold in the British Library. Among a number of finds from Anglo-Saxon Winchester, the City Museum has an exquisite tenth-century carved ivory panel depicting two angels, possibly a fragment of a much larger casket. The historic core itself preserves well the layout of Alfred's *burh* within its repaired Roman walls.

### 80. Breamore

St Mary's is an Anglo-Saxon cruciform church of about 1000 but now minus its northern transept arm and with a chancel rebuilt on the old foundations. Walls are of flint and 'long-and-short' quoins, with some original but mainly later windows. A squat but massive central tower is carried on crossing arches. On one of these arches, that of the south transept, is a carved inscription reading 'HER S WUTELATH SEO GECWYDRÆDNES THE' – 'Here the Word [or Covenant] is revealed unto thee'. As at Kirkdale in chapter 1, the inscription incorporates the OE characters Ð (*th*) and ƿ (*w*) but, more so than the Kirkdale example, it also shows how very different from modern English is Old English vocabulary and grammatical structure. Over the south door is a stone rood. Sadly, this was badly mutilated in the Reformation, as was another in the church of St Swithin at Headbourne Worthy, Winchester. Fortunately, that fate did not befall a high-quality Crucifixion carving in the abbey church of St Mary and St Ethelflæda at Romsey. Believed to have been a gift of King Edgar to a predecessor nunnery in 967, this is considered to be the oldest such carving in the country.

### 81. Corhampton

Described as a perfect little Saxon church in the *Collins Guide to English Parish Churches* (ed. John Betjeman, 1958), Corhampton's is of the early eleventh century and has many of its original architectural features remaining. Further south in the countryside at Boarhunt is another late small church of two cells, i.e. nave and chancel, with double-splayed windows and blocked-up doorway.

St Mary, Breamore: transept arch and the OE inscription. (*Steve Boxall*)

## BERKSHIRE

### 82. *Assandun*

The ancient county of Berkshire does not retain much of a physical nature from Anglo-Saxon times. Nonetheless, it has a crucial place in Anglo-Saxon history, and English history in general. For here in *Berrucscir*, in an as-yet unlocated royal hall at Wantage in 849, was born Alfred. Here too, charging 'with the rush of wild boar' at the Viking army twenty-one years later, Alfred began his rise to greatness. The site of the battle of Ash Down – from OE *ascen* (ash tree) and *dun* (hill) – is not precisely known. This is a common name, as already noted in chapter 3 for a subsequent battle in Essex. It is believed to have been in the chalk downs a few miles west of Alfred's birthplace, probably close to the already ancient hill fort and white horse at Uffington and where the names Ashbury and Ashdown House may also be clues.

Wantage, Uffington, Ashbury and much else are now in Oxfordshire, but on this occasion the 1974 boundary changes are being ignored. Berrucscir it was in Alfred's time, and that will suffice for this book.

### 83. Wickham

The Victorian church at Wickham retains a large, late Anglo-Saxon tower, itself topped by a nineteenth-century belfry. At almost 1,000 years separation in age, Wickham shares with Hovingham in Yorkshire what must be the record for reuse of an old tower in a new church. Old and new, built of flint, blend so well that the difference in age might come as a surprise.

## WILTSHIRE

### 84. Bradford-on-Avon

The church of St Lawrence is one of the most notable Anglo-Saxon churches. Virtually unaltered and without later inserted windows, the mystery of an interior dimly lit by small, double-splayed windows is easier to understand than in most survivors. A church was founded at the 'broad ford' in the bottom of the Avon valley by St Aldhelm, abbot of Malmesbury and first incumbent of the Bishopric of Sherborne established by King Ine of Wessex in 705. The present building at Bradford, although mostly dating from about 920, is thought to incorporate the foundations and perhaps other fabric of this older church. It is another small but tall church, its nave measuring 7.6 by 4 by 7.5 metres and the chancel 4 by 3 by 5.5. The chancel arch is a mere 1 metre in width. A transept, or porticus, survives on the north side. A south porticus has gone, but its narrow archway from the nave now forms the south door to the church. Otherwise unadorned, the interior has two sculpted angels of late tenth-century date and probably part of a now-lost larger sculpture. Despite its small size, the church nevertheless gives the impression of bold solidity thanks to construction in large ashlared limestone blocks and, uniquely, a continuous arcade of blind arches. This blind arcade, which girdles the building at a uniform height, is the earliest appearance in Britain of a feature that later became a common element of Romanesque architecture.

Like Jarrow-Wearmouth, Aldhelm's Malmesbury was a major monastic centre of learning and he, like Bede and Alcuin, an eminent religious writer and teacher. Slightly earlier than Bede, he was buried here in 709. In contrast to its Northumbrian counterpart, nothing remains of the early monastery, nor does anything survive from its rebuilding by King Athelstan in the 920s, in which he too was interred. How far that king's much later effigy in the present abbey church is

*Above left:* St Lawrence, 'the Saxon Church', Bradford-upon-Avon. (*Bryan Harris*)

*Above right:* Cross shaft, Codford St Peter: man harvesting grapes. (*Steve Boxall*)

a true likeness is unclear. The imposing hill-top setting, on the other hand, clearly reveals why his grandfather chose Malmesbury as one of his fortified *burhs*. The town's royal charter, also granted by Alfred, is the earliest in England.

**85. Britford**

Surviving Anglo-Saxon work in this church is limited but includes a crossing arch faced with bands of foliate decoration. This is a rare survival *in situ* of stone carving as an architectural element and shows how churches where some loose fragments survive, such as Jarrow, and probably many others, might once have been embellished. It is from the first half of the ninth century. Elsewhere in Wiltshire, the church at Codford St Peter has a substantial portion of a late ninth-century cross shaft. Standing 1.2 metres high, it depicts a man reaching up to grasp grapes from a vine and holding in his other hand what might be a wine flagon. This is thought to be symbolic of the blood of Christ and may be part of a depiction of the Eucharist. The man's tunic is of interest. Ramsbury, which briefly in the tenth century served a see for Wiltshire, has another partial cross shaft, this with well-preserved interlace.

**86. *Ethandun***

Despite the victory of Ethelred I and Alfred his brother at Ashdown in Berkshire, by 878 Alfred, now king, was stockaded at Athelney in what then were the undrained Somerset levels – Athelney meaning 'prince's island'. Incredibly, Alfred mustered a new army, sallied forth and at *Ethandun* surprised and so routed the army of Viking leader Guthrum that he made peace, withdrew from Wessex and, with Alfred himself standing as sponsor, converted to Christianity. Many another Viking leader and Viking army stood between Alfred's victory and the coronation of his great-grandson Edgar as king of the English in 973, but *Ethandun* proved decisive. The favoured interpretation of the name is the downs above the village of Edington in south-west Wiltshire.

## DORSETSHIRE

As is the case with neighbouring Somerset and Devon, 'shire' is not commonly applied to the county name these days. This in effect is going back to an older Anglo-Saxon form, *Dornsæta*, although *Dorseteschire* was in use by the tenth century. OE *sætna*, the 'set' in Dorset and Somerset, is our modern word 'settler', so the two county names refer to the settlers or dwellers around the places that are now called Dorchester and Somerton. They are the main survivors of what had been a widespread means of naming localities. For example, the OE originals of the names Chilterns and Peak District incorporated *sætna*.

**87. Wareham**

In the forefront of Viking sea-borne attack, Wareham was captured by Guthrum in 877 prior to the campaign that Alfred brought to a halt at Edington. Alfred subsequently made it one of his fortified boroughs and good traces of defensive earth ramparts can be seen. The banks, on three sides with the river forming the fourth side, had a total length of 1¼ miles. Wareham's other Anglo-Saxon survival dates from about 1030, this the compact church of St Martin atop the ramparts. The church consists of nave with later north aisle, chancel, three-storey porch and characteristic Anglo-Saxon double-splayed window. It is a tall building in typical Anglo-Saxon fashion, the nave being almost as tall as it is long. Inside is the effigy of another, much later warrior hero, T. E. Lawrence, who was instrumental in the church's restoration in the 1930s. Of Anglo-Saxon traces elsewhere in Dorset, the church at Winterbourne Steepleton has a tenth-century carved angel on one of its walls and that at Melbury Bubb contains an exceptional font depicting intertwined animals, very likely to be a reuse upside down of portions of a round cross shaft. A surviving portion of an elaborate tenth-century cross shaft from East Stour is kept by the British Museum.

Part of cross shaft from East Stour, now in the British Museum: interlace and acanthus scroll decoration. (*Steve Boxall*)

## SOMERSET

### 88. Bath

The present sixteenth-century abbey church had two predecessors, one of the twelfth century and one of the ninth. It was within the earliest of the three that King Edgar of Wessex was crowned the first king of unified England, his coronation being conducted by one of the foremost Anglo-Saxon archbishops, St Dunstan. That event is commemorated by a modern stone memorial within the current building. It records that 'ON THE NINTH DAY OF AUGUST AD1973 THE QUEEN AND THE DUKE OF EDINBURGH GAVE THANKS HERE FOR ONE THOUSAND YEARS OF THE ENGLISH MONARCHY SINCE THE CORONATION OF KING EDGAR ON WHIT SUNDAY AD 973 IN THE SAXON ABBEY ON THIS SITE'. Recalling the church inscriptions in eleventh-century English at Breamore and Kirkdale, it is interesting to speculate what this one might read like to an English speaker after another nine or ten centuries have elapsed – assuming it, too, survives that long.

### 89. Glastonbury

As at Bath and Malmesbury, nothing of the Anglo-Saxon monastery is now visible, but excavation beneath the ruins of its successor has revealed foundations dating from the end of the seventh century through to the middle of the tenth. Founded on an earlier Celtic Christian site by King Ine, Glastonbury became another major Anglo-Saxon monastic centre. Dunstan, a leading figure in the tenth-century Benedictine revival of monasticism after 100 years of decline and destruction, was abbot here. Here too was buried his patron, King Edgar.

## DEVON

### 90. Exeter

*Exanceaster*, the former 'Roman fort of the Exe', achieved its status as a cathedral city only in 1050, when the seat of the bishopric for *Defnascir*, or Devonshire, was transferred to it from Crediton. As his new episcopal base, the first Bishop of Exeter, Leofric, used a church that had been founded and richly endowed by King Athelstan over 100 years before. Although that church survives only in archaeological excavation and nothing above ground now dates from before 1133, Exeter Cathedral does retain something from its Anglo-Saxon past, the Exeter Book. An anthology of dozens of poems and riddles copied down by a single scribe somewhere in Wessex in about 960, this damaged but immensely important manuscript was gifted by Leofric himself. It is one of the three main sources of Anglo-Saxon poetry in England – a fourth is in Vercelli Cathedral, Italy – and the largest single collection. It contains both religious and secular poetry, including poems from the first centuries of Anglo-Saxon England such as *The Far Traveller* and *The Wanderer*. The manuscript is on display in the Cathedral Library and can be viewed on request.

The Cathedral Library is housed in the Bishop's House in the precinct: check opening hours. The Exeter Book is just one of 6,000 manuscripts and 20,000 printed books in the library.

### 91. Sidbury

The church of St Peter and St Giles has a small Anglo-Saxon crypt, all above being late twelfth-century to fourteenth-century. The crypt is the fifth and last to be featured in this book – see also Hexham and Ripon, chapter 1, Repton and Wing, chapter 2. A little way to the north, inside the church of St Andrew at Colyton, is a re-erected shaft and partial head of a high cross. As with the portion of the East Stour Cross from Dorset, this has tenth-century entwined acanthus foliage and bird carving.

## CORNWALL

### 92. Crosses

Cornwall, the last remnant of British Dumnonia, retained its autonomy into the ninth century. Churches and town names dedicated to saints of the early British Church, particularly the further west one goes, together with place names of Celtic origin and the survival into the seventeenth century of spoken Cornish, reflect the late takeover by Anglo-Saxon Wessex. Also demonstrating native continuity, the churchyard of St Fecitas at Phillack in the west of the county has a complete high cross of about AD 1000, with a wheel-head and plait work decoration in the Celtic tradition. Of other crosses, the tenth-century shaft outside the church at St Neots is a richly carved cross in granite. Although much shortened, it still shows bold bands of interlace on all four sides. Cardinham, with its English rather than Celtic name, possesses another cross of tenth-century date outside its church.

## SURREY

### 93. Stoke D'Abernon

Of the small number of Surrey churches with Anglo-Saxon parts, St Mary's at

Stoke has some walling and a sundial. St Mary, Guildford, and St Nicholas, Compton, have late towers.

## EAST AND WEST SUSSEX

### 94. Battle

William the Conqueror's abbey and an Old French place-name origin announce Battle as a Norman site, but it is an Anglo-Saxon site too. For here, on 14 October 1066, took place the battle between King Harold's 'shield wall' and Duke William's cavalry and archers. To the English, it was Senlac Hill. To posterity, the encounter is better known by the name of the town of Hastings seven miles to the south. To the Normans, it became known simply as *La Batailge*. Built in thanksgiving for his victory, Battle Abbey was William's first religious foundation in England. Although recent investigation suggests the battlefield lies under the modern village rather than on the open hillside running southwards, as long assumed, the site of the abbey's high altar is the reputed spot where Harold fell, two of his brothers and many good men, as the *Anglo-Saxon Chronicle* called them, by his side. Standing on that spot in the now-ruined church, ponder for a moment on subsequent British history had a finely balanced battle whose final outcome was resolved by an element of chance ended differently.

An English Heritage exhibition and audio tour provide a grounding in the battle and its context. If visiting that unique pictorial Norman version of events, the Bayeux Tapestry, bear in mind that it was embroidered by Anglo-Saxon women, in all probability was designed by an Anglo-Saxon artist, and continued an Anglo-Saxon tradition of hanging pictorial tapestries on the walls of great timber halls.

## THE NORMAN CONQUEST AND THE MODERN MONARCHY

Earl Harold Godwinson of Wessex, crowned King Harold II on 6 January 1066 in succession to Edward the Confessor, was the last Anglo-Saxon king. Confronted by battle-hardened foreign claimants who coveted England's crown and prosperity, he defeated King Harald Hardrada and his Norwegian army at the Battle of Stamford Bridge, near York, but three weeks later succumbed to Duke William and his Norman-Breton army on

Senlac Hill. Watershed though these few weeks in 1066 were, Anglo-Saxon royal blood from the direct line going back to Alfred, Egbert and beyond was carried forward into England's post-Conquest monarchy by the marriage of Edmund Ironside's granddaughter, Margaret, to Malcolm III of Scotland and the marriage in turn of a daughter of that union to Henry I of England, the Conqueror's youngest son. That Wessex blood remains in the modern British monarchy through its descent from both Henry I and Saint Margaret's son, David I of Scotland. Remarkably, via the marriage of a daughter to a future Grand Prince of Kiev, so does Harold's.

Silver penny of King Harold II, 1066. (*AMR Coins*)

**95. Worth**

The handsome church of St Nicholas was built in the tenth century and into the eleventh, its tower and spire being nineteenth-century but built in keeping with the rest. It is one of the most complete and important late Anglo-Saxon churches still in existence. Other than the tower and a south porch, the church possesses a ground plan that has not been subjected to subsequent extension or alteration. A rare apsidal chancel/sanctuary is the only standing example in Wessex and has a domed roof. Bold pilaster strips and string courses punctuate the walls externally. Entry is via an unusually tall south doorway. The chancel arch, at 6.7 metres in height and 4.3 in width, is one of the largest and finest Anglo-Saxon arches. Although later windows have been inserted, the nave is still partly lit by three original deeply-splayed, round-headed double windows high in the walls and the

St Nicholas, Worth. *Above:* External view of the east end. *Right:* Internal view showing apse, chancel arch and transept arches. (*Bill Puttick, St Nicholas Parish*)

apse by single splayed windows. The church retains its north and south transepts, each opening from the nave via substantial arches. The modern nave roof is a replacement following a major fire in 1986.

Worth is a common OE place-name ending in Mercian England, where it meant an enclosure. Here, however, it comes from the personal name Wurth, as does Worthing.

### PLACE NAMES 4: *ING* AND *INGHAM*

Thousands of Old English place names tell of a mainly agrarian society. Honiton, for example, is Huna's farmstead. Many names are based on the bond between a local leader and populace. Hastings and Worthing are just two of numerous examples of tribal *ingas* names, meaning respectively Hæsta's people and Wurth's people. Other examples in this book include Birmingham, or Beorma's people's village. Ovingham in Northumberland is Offa's people's village, but a different Offa to the Mercian king. Wittering was listed in Domesday Book as Witeringham but has since lost the *ham* element. The name Sompting also comes from a group of people but is slightly different. Here it does not refer to a person but derives from *sumptingas*, or 'people of the marsh'. This alludes to the low-lying land below the town and in Anglo-Saxon times prone to flooding. Note in the name the modern word sump, marshland effectively being a drainage sump.

**96. Sompting**

Sompting's church of St Mary was rebuilt by the Knights Templar in the thirteenth century but retains portions of two frieze carvings of saints and, most importantly, an Anglo-Saxon tower dating from the early eleventh century. This is England's only original helm tower of the type more familiar in Germany's Rhineland; there are other examples but they are much younger, often Victorian. This type of tower is crowned by four sloping, diamond-shaped roof sections placed between the pointed gables of its four walls. The resulting pyramid shape was the precursor of true church spires. What is exceptional here is that, beneath replacement oak roofing shingles, the original timbers remain. The tower is constructed from

St Mary, Sompting: the Rhenish tower. (*Steve Boxall*)

cobbles and flint and incorporates round-headed belfry openings with baluster shafts, small triangular-headed windows and pilaster strips through the full height of the walls. It is 30 metres tall.

**97. Bosham**

There are at least another half-dozen Sussex churches with substantial Anglo-Saxon fabric, including Clayton. Of them, Holy Trinity at Bosham has an unrivalled distinction, for it is depicted, with Earl (later King) Harold entering, on the Bayeux Tapestry. It still has the nave walls and tower of that building, the latter topped by a later broached spire, and the chancel arch, which is identifiable in the Tapestry scene. The next scene depicts Earl Harold setting out on the ill-fated voyage from Bosham's harbour that was to land him in the clutches of Duke William.

## KENT

**98. Lyminge**

The church of St Mary and St Ethelburga was founded as a double monastery for women and men by Ethelburga, daughter of King Ethelbert of Kent (*c.* 560–616) and widow of King Edwin of Northumbria (killed in battle, 633). Although considerably altered, the present church retains some structure from the later Anglo-Saxon period, including round-headed windows. Earlier times at Lyminge, possibly the time of Ethelbert and Ethelburga themselves, dramatically came to life in 2012 with the archaeological discovery of the footprint of a great hall. Still with the trenches and post-pits that held planked walls and monumental timber entrances, the footprint is 21.3 metres in length. Together with earlier excavations elsewhere, including Yeavering near Bamburgh in Edwin's own kingdom, the archaeological evidence here provides a good picture of the communal royal halls portrayed in *Beowulf*.

**99. Minster-in-Sheppey**

The 'ey' in Sheppey is a remnant of OE *egland*, or island, as it also is in Athelney in Somerset. As in the case of the church at Lyminge, the 'church of the island of sheep' was founded by a royal daughter, in its case by Saxburg, daughter of a subsequent King of Kent in about 670. Dedicated to St Mary and St Saxburg herself, it was originally a nunnery. Surviving Anglo-Saxon fabric, including massive tower, is largely composed of Roman tile bricks but much of the church is of later date.

**100. Canterbury *Cantwaraburg***

Sharing the title of Cradle of Christianity in England, Canterbury closes this guide just as Lindisfarne opened it. It was to Canterbury that King Ethelbert of Kent invited St Augustine and his companions following their disembarkation on Thanet in 597. Bede's *Ecclesiastical History* tells of Ethelbert's Frankish Christian queen, Bertha, worshipping at a Canterbury church dedicated to St Martin of Tours, and of Augustine going there to preach. The present St Martin's stands a quarter mile to the east of the town walls, which accords with Bede placing of the queen's church on the east side of the town. Ancient brick structure seen in the south wall and blocked doorway of its chancel also accords with Bede's statement that the church dated from the Roman occupation. It was probably restored rather than surviving intact. This would seem, then, to be the building known to Augustine over 1,400 years ago. Added soon afterwards, St Martin's nave is dated to the early seventh century. It was built of salvaged Roman bricks and stones, most easily seen externally and in the west wall internally. The church was much altered in the thirteenth and fourteenth centuries, with a west tower being added and the chancel extended eastwards as well. Most original architectural features have been obliterated as a result. Nevertheless, to enter St Martin's is to enter the oldest church in Britain.

Bede also recorded the establishment within the town walls of Augustine's episcopal church, Christ Church, seat of the first English bishopric and archbishopric (OE *arcebiscroprice*). He also wrote of the founding of a monastery dedicated to saints Peter and Paul a short distance outside the walls. That was in 602. Both were extended and partially rebuilt over the next 400 years, growing into large cloistered complexes and constituting another major centre of learning in Anglo-Saxon England. The period of monastic reform and revival under Archbishop Dunstan in the second half of the tenth century also saw St Peter's and St Paul's rededicated to Augustine himself.

Of the Anglo-Saxon Christ Church, nothing visible is revealed by the current cathedral still dedicated to Christ, although it is known through archaeological investigation that in its final form it was about 76 metres long. It was destroyed by fire in 1067. Of the monastery, just a few traces are exposed among the more extensive ruins of St Augustine's Norman replacement. These do, however, include some of the earliest structure and the roofless crypt of a massive rotunda tower begun by Abbot Wulfric in 1050, plus the locations of the tombs of Augustine, Ethelbert and some of their successors. The English Heritage guidebook and on-site visitor centre give a good idea of what the Anglo-Saxon abbey was like. The Canterbury Heritage Museum also has Kentish artefacts, including a gold and garnet cloisonné pendant.

As at Lindisfarne and Winchester, Anglo-Saxon Canterbury is better preserved in a form other than stone: the illuminated manuscripts made in its scriptoria and now in the British Library. Additionally, two stunning manuscript codices abroad reveal the achievements of Canterbury and Minster-in-Thanet scriptoria across the Anglo-Saxon age. One, an illuminated Gospel book of the mid-eighth century known as the Codex Aureus, is an acknowledged masterpiece of manuscript production and, alongside the Lindisfarne Gospels, foremost of the early mediaeval luxury manuscripts of Anglo-Saxon England. Although sharing some of the features of Insular art, it is more Continental in appearance than its Northumbrian counterpart. Of additional interest is an inscription recording that a local ealdorman and his wife purchased it back from plundering Vikings and returned it to Christ Church – though it has ended up in Scandinavia nonetheless. It is now in the Royal Library, Stockholm. From much later, about 1020, the Eadwig Gospels in Hanover's August Kestner Museum is the culmination of three centuries of Anglo-Saxon illumination. Like the Lindisfarne Gospels, it is one of the few manuscript books of which anything is known of the maker, in its case the Christ Church scribe and (probable) artist after whom it is named.

St Martin's church, the cathedral and the abbey are grouped together as a World Heritage Site. The abbey ruins are in the guardianship of English Heritage.

*Left:* St Augustine's Abbey: seventh-century foundations with markers to the graves of early bishops of Canterbury.

*Below:* St Augustine's Abbey: interpretive board showing the ground plan and possible appearance of the original monastery of St Peter and St Paul. (© *Photograph reproduced with the permission of English Heritage*)

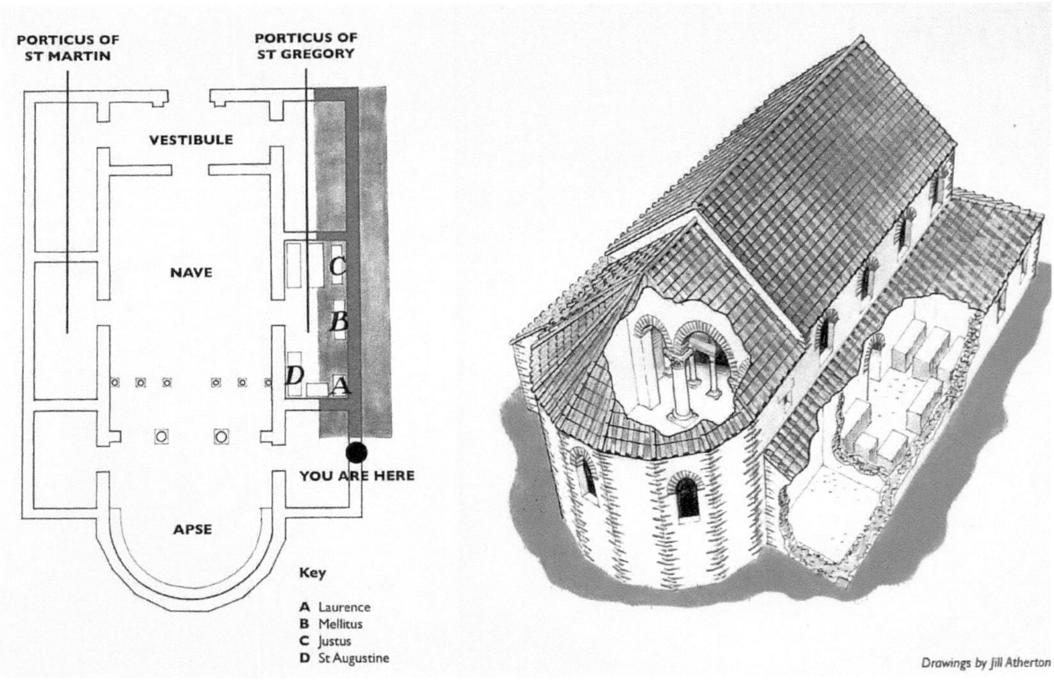